GLENCOE

M000300136

VOCABULARY BUILDER

Peter Fischer, Editorial Consultant

National-Louis University

Course 3

 **Glencoe**

New York, New York   Columbus, Ohio   Chicago, Illinois   Peoria, Illinois   Woodland Hills, California

Acknowledgments

The pronunciation key used in the glossary has been reproduced by permission
from *The American Heritage Dictionary of the English Language, Fourth Edition*.
Copyright © 2000 by Houghton Mifflin Company.

Printed in the United States of America

Send all inquiries to:
Glencoe/McGraw-Hill
8787 Orion Place
Columbus, OH 43240

SE ISBN: 0-07-861664-6
ATE ISBN: 0-07-861665-4

5 6 7 8 9 10 113 10 09 08 07

Contents

Name _____

The Headless Horseman of Sleepy Hollow

In the peaceful valley of Sleepy Hollow lived a tall, thin schoolteacher named Ichabod Crane. His skinny arms **protruded** from
tattered sleeves, and his tiny head was **bedecked** with two huge
ears and a large, narrow nose. Some said Ichabod Crane actually
5 looked like a crane. Yet Ichabod was a good teacher. He rarely
whipped the children, and sometimes he even walked them home.
This is how he met the lovely Katrina Van Tassel, the daughter
of a farmer. She was not only pretty, she was rich. Ichabod was
soon **enchanted** by her charms. Day and night, Ichabod's mind
10 **invariably** drifted to Katrina's beauty and her father's rich farm.

However, there was another man in the village who was also
in love with Katrina. His name was Brom Van Brunt, but every–
one called him Brom Bones. Unlike Ichabod, Brom was strong
and muscular. The villagers often marveled over his **brawny**
15 **physique.** Ichabod feared Brom Bones, so to **disguise** his
amorous purposes, Ichabod pretended to give Katrina singing
lessons.

Brom was not fooled, but whenever he challenged Ichabod
to a fight, Ichabod refused. Brom, therefore, began playing tricks
20 on Ichabod. He stopped up Ichabod's chimney and **ransacked**
his house, upsetting his furniture and leaving a mess. Then one
day Ichabod got an invitation to a party at Katrina's house. Brom
Bones was also invited. Ichabod was an **accomplished** dancer
and danced every dance with Katrina while Brom Bones stared at
25 him with rage in his eyes. When the dancing ended, the men began
telling ghost stories about a headless ghost who rode about the
valley. Ichabod believed the stories, so as he nervously rode home
that dark, lonely night, he jumped at the slightest sound and hid
from every shadow. In the darkest part of the woods, he heard the
30 sound of a horse and rider behind him. Shaking wildly, Ichabod
finally peeked over his high collar. What he saw sent a shiver
through his body. It was a headless horseman, carrying his head
under his arm. Ichabod spurred his horse into a gallop, but it was
too late. The headless rider lifted his head and threw it at Ichabod.
35 The next morning the schoolteacher was not at school. He had
disappeared. In the woods the townspeople found only Ichabod's
hat and a broken pumpkin. Not long after this Brom Bones married
Katrina. When asked about the pumpkin and what happened in
the woods that night, Brom Bones would just laugh.

Words

accomplished

amorous

bedeck

brawny

disguise

enchanted

invariably

physique

protrude

ransack

Each word in this lesson's word list appears in dark type in the selection you just read. Think about how the vocabulary word is used in the selection, then write the letter for the best answer to each question.

1. If something *protrudes* (line 2), it _____.
   (A) injures slightly   (B) sticks out
   (C) causes laughter   (D) is the source of admiration

   1. _____

2. Which word could best replace *bedecked* in line 3?
   (A) dampened   (B) alarmed
   (C) replaced   (D) decorated

   2. _____

3. If someone is *enchanted* (line 9), he or she is _____.
   (A) under a spell   (B) singing a song
   (C) sleeping soundly   (D) suffering from a disease

   3. _____

4. If something *invariably* (line 10) happens, it _____.
   (A) rarely occurs   (B) goes on constantly without change
   (C) cannot be counted on   (D) cannot be seen

   4. _____

5. A *brawny* (line 14) person is _____.
   (A) quiet   (B) musically talented
   (C) strong and muscular   (D) intelligent

   5. _____

6. Which words best define the word *physique* (line 15)?
   (A) mental ability   (B) the appearance of the body
   (C) medical history   (D) religious beliefs

   6. _____

7. If you *disguise* (line 15) something, you _____.
   (A) put it in plain view   (B) destroy it
   (C) strongly dislike it   (D) hide its appearance

   7. _____

8. An *amorous* (line 16) purpose is one that involves _____.
   (A) love   (B) money
   (C) danger   (D) music

   8. _____

9. If you *ransack* (line 20) something, you _____.
   (A) surround it   (B) rebuilt it
   (C) search it thoroughly   (D) move it from place to place

   9. _____

10. An *accomplished* (line 23) dancer is _____.
    (A) clumsy   (B) unable to get a partner
    (C) skillful   (D) poorly dressed

    10. _____

Applying Meaning

Decide which word in parentheses best completes the sentence. Then write the sentence, adding the missing word.

1. José finally overcame his shyness and wrote a(n) _____ poem to Maria. (amorous; brawny)

   _____

   _____

   _____

2. Willard was such an _____ chess player, he could play and win ten matches at the same time. (accomplished; enchanted)

   _____

   _____

   _____

3. Returning from a long trip, we found someone had _____ our apartment and broken my favorite lamp. (disguised; ransacked)

   _____

   _____

   _____

4. Every year at Christmas, our village is _____ with colorful lights and banners. (bedecked; ransacked)

   _____

   _____

   _____

5. The football player's _____ body could not be hidden under his size XXXL uniform. (brawny; enchanted)

   _____

   _____

   _____

Read each sentence or short passage below. Write "correct" on the answer line if the vocabulary word has been used correctly or "incorrect" if it has been used incorrectly.

6. Because of the expected cold weather, orange growers took several steps to *protrude* their crop.

6. _____

7. Whenever there was work to be done around the house, Josh *invariably* remembered some homework he had to do.

7. _____

8. In Mr. Hanson's class we studied gravity and other laws of *physiques*.

8. _____

9. The fairy tale took place in an *enchanted* forest full of elves and wizards.

9. _____

10. Many of Shakespeare's plays include comic scenes in which a character *disguises* his appearance to spy on someone.

10. _____

For each word used incorrectly, write a sentence using the word properly.

_____

_____

_____

_____

_____

Mastering Meaning

Imagine that you are a reporter for the *Sleepy Hollow Gazette*. Write a newspaper account of the mysterious disappearance of Ichabod Crane. Include quotes from Katrina and Brom Van Brunt. Mention the rumors that both Mr. Crane and Mr. Van Brunt were in love with Katrina and the events at the party the night before Ichabod's disappearance. Keep your report factual and objective. Be sure to include the *who, what, where, when,* and possible *why* of Mr. Crane's disappearance. Use some of the words you studied in this lesson.

Name _____

Our moods affect the way we act. It is not difficult to tell if someone is unhappy over criticism or upset with a grade on a paper. It shows in the individual's face, in movements, and in actions. While each of us is unique, moods and behaviors generally fall into clear categories. The words in this lesson describe certain moods and behaviors you will probably recognize in yourself and in others.

Words
amicable
berserk
defiant
despondent
disgruntled
exuberant
lascivious
loathsome
meddlesome
melancholy

Unlocking Meaning

Read the sentences or short passages below. Write the letter for the correct definition of the italicized vocabulary word.

1. Sandy cannot stand her cousin Jasper. Whenever Jasper visits, he always gets to watch the TV shows he likes and to sit in her favorite chair. Nevertheless, Sandy's mother makes her behave in an *amicable* manner because Jasper is, after all, a relative.
   (A) rude   (B) loud
   (C) friendly   (D) sneaky

2. Coach Santos is usually quite calm and relaxed, but when the umpire threw his star player out of the game, he went *berserk*. Coach threw his hat on the field, kicked dirt into the air, and refused to leave the playing field.
   (A) into a wild rage   (B) quiet
   (C) relaxed and comfortable (D) happy

3. The more the police demanded the criminal's surrender, the more *defiant* he became. At one point he shook his fist at the officers and dared them to come and get him.
   (A) generous   (B) resistant and unyielding
   (C) sneaky   (D) foolish

4. After his ideas were turned down by the group, Mike became *despondent*. He said little and left the meeting early.
   (A) excited   (B) angry
   (C) encouraged   (D) discouraged

5. Four *disgruntled* workers walked off the job when the layoffs were announced. For weeks they had been unhappy, but when their friends and coworkers lost their jobs, they took action.
   (A) tired   (B) simple
   (C) very displeased   (D) amazed

1. _____

2. _____

3. _____

4. _____

5. _____

6. On the last day of the school year, a crowd of *exuberant* students gathered at the door waiting for the final bell to ring. When the bell finally rang, their cheers could be heard blocks away.
   (A) wildly joyful   (B) slow moving
   (C) intelligent   (D) confident

6. _____

7. The city council passed a law to prevent stores from displaying *lascivious* books and magazines where young children might see them. Such material was felt to be improper for them.
   (A) tattered and torn   (B) containing sexual material
   (C) educationally sound   (D) costly

7. _____

8. We were stunned when the bully took the child's bike and lunch box. We hardly knew what to do since we had never seen such *loathsome* behavior before.
   (A) humorous   (B) surprising
   (C) extremely hateful   (D) lazy

8. _____

9. Hal had grown weary of Kim's *meddlesome* behavior. Her constant questions about his personal life were getting quite annoying.
   (A) charming   (B) athletic
   (C) simple   (D) interfering

9. _____

10. Tears appeared in the eyes of several graduates when the *melancholy* notes of the school song were played. They knew they were saying good-bye to their carefree school days.
    (A) sad   (B) religious
    (C) happy   (D) piercing

10. _____

Applying Meaning

Decide which word in parentheses best completes the sentence. Then write the sentence, adding the missing word.

1. In many cities it is illegal to display _____ magazines or other vulgar material where children might see them. (amicable; lascivious)

_____

_____

_____

2. Kwan had been _____ for days because he was sure he had failed the test. (despondent; exuberant)

_____

_____

_____

3. However, when he saw that he had earned an A, Kwan became _____ and danced down the hall.

_____

_____

_____

4. Refusing the blindfold, the condemned traitor faced the firing squad with a _____ stare. (defiant; meddlesome)

_____

_____

5. Recalling his happy childhood, the elderly man began to feel a little _____ . (disgruntled; melancholy)

_____

_____

_____

6. The heat and humidity caused the dog to go _____ : it ran in circles and growled at everyone. (amicable; berserk)

_____

_____

_____

7. Destroying the computers and painting racial slurs on the walls
   was a _____ act of vandalism. (loathsome; meddlesome)

   _____

   _____

   _____

8. Even after days of talks, the strikers failed to reach an _____
   agreement with management. (amicable; exuberant)

   _____

   _____

   _____

9. In this book a _____ woman constantly tries to make romantic
   matches among her friends. (despondent; meddlesome)

   _____

   _____

   _____

10. The plant had to close because a few _____ workers locked them-
    selves to the main gate. (disgruntled; melancholy)

    _____

    _____

    _____

Cultural Literacy Note

The Humours

An old theory held that the human body was made up of four liquids,
or humours: blood, phlegm, yellow bile, and black bile. One's personal-
ity was thought to be the result of these liquids. Someone who seemed
sentimental and thoughtful was thought to have too much black bile.
People of this type were called *melancholy*, a word formed from the
Greek word *melas*, meaning "black," and *khole*, meaning "bile."

Do Some Research: Look up the meaning and history of these words:
sanguine, choleric, and *phlegmatic.*

Name _____

The Latin word *pellere* means "to drive" or "to push." It appears in several forms in English words, yet each form still keeps some hint of its original Latin meaning. It most often occurs as *-pel-*, as in the word *compel*. However, it sometimes becomes *-peal-* as in *appeal*, or *-pul-* as in *pulse*. Being able to recognize this root will help you unlock the meaning of a number of unfamiliar words. Each vocabulary word in this lesson has some form of the Latin word *pellere*.

Root	Meaning	English Word
-pel-	to drive, to push	compel
-peal-		appeal
-pul-		pulse

Words

- **appeal**
- **compel**
- **expel**
- **impulse**
- **peal**
- **propel**
- **propulsion**
- **pulse**
- **repeal**
- **repulse**

Unlocking Meaning

A vocabulary word appears in italics in each sentence or short passage below. Find the root in the vocabulary word and think about how the word is used in the passage. Then write a definition for the vocabulary word. Compare your definition with the definition in the dictionary in the back of the book.

1. To make it easier to reach those injured by the tornado, the mayor made an *appeal* for others to stay out of the area.

   _____

   _____

   _____

2. The new state regulation will *compel* all twelfth-grade students to pass tests in reading and math in order to graduate.

   _____

   _____

   _____

3. The lifeguard was able to *expel* the water from the victim's lungs. After that, her breathing became easier.

   _____

   _____

   _____

4. Seeing the beautiful ocean waves pounding on the shore, I gave in to a sudden *impulse* and dashed fully clothed into the surf.

_____

_____

_____

5. As the monument to the dead firefighters was unveiled, the *peal* of a single church bell broke the solemn quiet.

_____

_____

_____

6. A powerful engine *propels* a jet ski by taking in water at the front of the craft and rapidly forcing it out behind.

_____

_____

_____

7. Before the steam engine, horses were the most important means of *propulsion*. They pulled everything from trolleys to plows.

_____

_____

_____

8. By pressing an artery in my neck, the doctor could feel my *pulse*.

_____

_____

_____

9. Angry voters organized a drive to *repeal* the tax increase. If put to a vote, the increase would surely go down to defeat.

_____

_____

_____

10. For days, the defenders of the Alamo were able to *repulse* every attack. On March 6, 1836, however, the mission was overrun.

_____

_____

_____

Applying Meaning

Read each sentence or short passage below. Write "correct" on the answer line if the vocabulary word has been used correctly or "incorrect" if it has been used incorrectly.

1. His work on the project earned him a *propulsion* to foreman.

2. The judge could not *compel* the witness to testify against himself.

3. The bells rang every evening at six o'clock. They would *repeal* two hours later at eight o'clock.

4. The losing candidate remained quite bitter. He always *repulsed* his old opponent's friendly approaches.

5. *Peals* of laughter filled the theater during the comedian's act.

6. It took every ounce of my strength to overcome the *pulse* to tell him what I thought of his rude behavior.

1. _____

2. _____

3. _____

4. _____

5. _____

6. _____

For each word used incorrectly, write a sentence using the word properly.

_____

_____

_____

_____

_____

_____

_____

_____

_____

_____

Follow the directions below to write a sentence using a vocabulary word.

7. Describe something you did. Use any form of the word *impulse*.

_____

_____

_____

8. Write a slogan for a worthy cause. Use any form of the word *appeal*.

_____

_____

_____

9. Describe how a bicycle works. Use any form of the word *propel*.

_____

_____

_____

10. Use any form of the word *expel* to describe something that happened at school.

_____

_____

_____

Spelling and Language

Adding -ed and -ing

When a one-syllable word ends with one vowel and one consonant, the final consonant is doubled before adding -ed or -ing. When a word of two or more syllables ends with one vowel and one consonant, the final consonant is doubled only if the final syllable is stressed.

skip	skipped	skipping
com**pel**	compelled	compelling
limit	limited	limiting

Add the Endings: Add *-ed* and *-ing* to these words: prefer, equal, shovel, bother, wonder, permit.

Name _____

How well do you remember the words you studied in Lessons 1 through 3? Take the following test covering the words from the last three lessons.

Part 1 Choose the Correct Meaning

Each question below includes a word in capital letters, followed by four words or phrases. Choose the word or phrase that is <u>closest</u> in meaning to the word in capital letters. Write the letter for your answer on the line provided.

Sample

| S. FINISH | (A) enjoy | (B) complete | S. _____**B**_____ |
| | (C) destroy | (D) enlarge | |

| 1. AMICABLE | (A) talented | (B) kindly | 1. _____ |
| | (C) unusual | (D) late | |

| 2. RANSACK | (A) damage | (B) put together | 2. _____ |
| | (C) forget | (D) believe | |

| 3. DESPONDENT | (A) without hope | (B) deep | 3. _____ |
| | (C) careful | (D) energetic | |

| 4. DISGRUNTLED | (A) noisy | (B) ugly | 4. _____ |
| | (C) talkative | (D) unhappy | |

| 5. INVARIABLY | (A) different | (B) thoughtfully | 5. _____ |
| | (C) skilled | (D) without change | |

| 6. EXUBERANT | (A) spirited | (B) cowardly | 6. _____ |
| | (C) uncovered | (D) forgetful | |

| 7. BRAWNY | (A) blonde | (B) muscular | 7. _____ |
| | (C) brave | (D) tan | |

| 8. LOATHSOME | (A) lazy | (B) wealthy | 8. _____ |
| | (C) hateful | (D) old | |

| 9. BEDECK | (A) extend | (B) overcome | 9. _____ |
| | (C) beat | (D) adorn | |

| 10. MEDDLESOME | (A) playful | (B) loud | 10. _____ |
| | (C) hardworking | (D) prying | |

11. IMPULSE   (A) urge   (B) smell   11. _____
                   (C) memory   (D) order

12. ENCHANTED   (A) long   (B) rhymed   12. _____
                   (C) spellbound   (D) religious

13. REPEAL   (A) harvest   (B) cancel   13. _____
                   (C) prepare   (D) save

14. COMPEL   (A) send   (B) encourage   14. _____
                   (C) advise   (D) force

15. PULSE   (A) excuse   (B) beat   15. _____
                   (C) sound   (D) smoothness

Part 2 Matching Words and Meanings

Match the definition in Column B with the word in Column A. Write the letter of the correct definition on the line provided.

Column A	Column B	
16. expel	a. to cause to move forward	16. _____
17. defiant	b. in a rage	17. _____
18. accomplished	c. the appearance of the body	18. _____
19. propel	d. very sad	19. _____
20. berserk	e. to hide	20. _____
21. appeal	f. unwilling to yield to authority	21. _____
22. disguise	g. skilled	22. _____
23. physique	h. hateful	23. _____
24. loathsome	i. request	24. _____
25. melancholy	j. to push out	25. _____

Name _____

Current Trends

Too often, young people prepare themselves for jobs that are rapidly disappearing. This **tendency** is not hard to understand. When people think about good jobs, they think about ones they have heard or read about. They may even have had some
5 experience with them. In other words they think about jobs that already exist.

However, the workplace keeps changing because the world keeps changing. Jobs in some fields are increasing, while those in other fields are disappearing. In the early part of this century,
10 manufacturing jobs **dominated** the Help Wanted ads in newspapers. Factories hired huge numbers of people and paid them good money to build everything from automobiles to paper clips. However, by the 1960s machines were doing the work men and women used to do. **Automation** greatly reduced the number of
15 manufacturing jobs. Moreover, businesses with factories requiring a large labor pool have moved to countries where labor is cheap. The number of manufacturing jobs available today is **insignificant** compared to those in other fields.

According to government figures, the **preponderance** of jobs
20 in the next century will be in service-related fields, such as health and business. Jobs will also be plentiful in the technical fields and in **retail** establishments, such as stores and restaurants. The **expansion** in these fields is due to several factors: an aging population, numerous technical breakthroughs, and our changing
25 lifestyles. The highest-paying jobs will go to people with degrees in science, computers, engineering, and health care.

What will employers of the future look for? Employers will want workers who are **flexible** and therefore able to change as business changes. The workers of the future will need to **tolerate** these
30 changes. Many people will be expected to perform **temporary** jobs, then move on to new and different tasks. Each new task may involve new skills and understandings. The only thing that will remain the same is change.

Words

automation

dominate

expansion

flexible

insignificant

preponderance

retail

temporary

tendency

tolerate

Each word in this lesson's word list appears in dark type in the selection you just read. Think about how the vocabulary word is used in the selection. Then write the letter for the best answer to each question.

1. A *tendency* (line 2) is a(n)
   (A) occupation   (B) trend or direction
   (C) agreement   (D) time of year

   1. _____

2. Which word could best replace *dominated* in line 10?
   (A) misplaced   (B) wrote
   (C) controlled   (D) hired

   2. _____

3. *Automation* (line 14) means the use of
   (A) machines to do work   (B) wheels to move equipment
   (C) factories instead of   (D) education
       small shops

   3. _____

4. Which word could best replace *insignificant* in line 17?
   (A) magnificent   (B) valuable
   (C) unimportant   (D) beautiful

   4. _____

5. Which word or words could best replace *preponderance* in line 19?
   (A) loss   (B) description
   (C) smallest number   (D) largest number

   5. _____

6. A *retail* (line 22) business is one that
   (A) buys land for development   (B) hires doctors
   (C) sells things in small,   (D) loans money to people
       individual amounts

   6. _____

7. *Expansion* (line 23) means
   (A) growth   (B) value
   (C) sale   (D) difficulty

   7. _____

8. If you are *flexible* (line 28), you can
   (A) be on time   (B) speak another language
   (C) work hard   (D) change to meet new conditions

   8. _____

9. In line 29, the word *tolerate* means
   (A) accept   (B) dislike
   (C) avoid   (D) talk about

   9. _____

10. A *temporary* (line 30) job is one that
    (A) requires skills   (B) lasts forever
    (C) is short-lived   (D) stops slowly

    10. _____

Applying Meaning

Write the vocabulary word or a form of the word that fits each clue below. Then use the word in a sentence.

1. An example would be a machine that fills bottles.

   _____

   _____

   _____

2. The leader of the wolf pack will do this to the other members of the pack.

   _____

   _____

   _____

3. Someone who can change plans at the last minute might be described with this word.

   _____

   _____

   _____

4. Things fitting this description will not last forever.

   _____

   _____

   _____

5. It has a prefix that means "not" and comes from the word "signify."

   _____

   _____

   _____

6. You see these kinds of stores in malls and shopping centers.

   _____

   _____

   _____

7. The greatest in number, weight, or importance.

_____

_____

_____

Decide which form of the word in parentheses best completes each
sentence. Then write the sentence, adding the missing word

8. A good education can _____ your chances of finding work.
   (expansion)

_____

_____

_____

9. I am very _____ of mistakes but not of lies. (tolerate)

_____

_____

_____

10. People in this neighborhood _____ to get along very well. (tendency)

_____

_____

_____

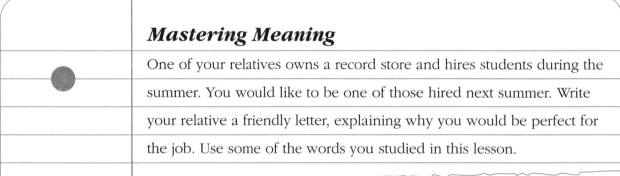

Mastering Meaning

One of your relatives owns a record store and hires students during the
summer. You would like to be one of those hired next summer. Write
your relative a friendly letter, explaining why you would be perfect for
the job. Use some of the words you studied in this lesson.

Vocabulary of Work and Workers

Name _____

Work is an important part of everyone's life. It is not surprising, therefore, that many of our words deal with work and workers. Supervisors need words to describe the levels of skills of the workers. Workers need words to define the work they do and how well they and others do it. In this lesson you will learn ten words that describe work and workers.

Unlocking Meaning

Read the sentences or short passages below. Write the letter for the correct definition of the italicized vocabulary word.

1. After graduating from a technical high school, John was eager to pursue a career as a plumber. To learn the trade, he became an *apprentice* so that he could learn from an experienced plumber.
   (A) partner in a business   (B) experienced supervisor
   (C) paid advisor   (D) someone learning a trade

2. Because of her natural *aptitude* for painting and drawing, Yolanda looked forward to a career as a commercial artist.
   (A) lack of interest   (B) curiosity
   (C) ability or talent   (D) fame

3. Carmen thought the job would give her the chance to use her creative talents. However, she soon learned that her job was *drudgery*, ordering supplies and answering the telephone.
   (A) unpleasant, dull work   (B) easy and fun
   (C) full of opportunities   (D) work requiring great
                                       personal skills

4. Building the cabinets required a knowledge of wood and exact measurements. Only a *journeyman* carpenter could be trusted with the job.
   (A) uneducated   (B) lazy
   (C) skillful and experienced   (D) unknown

5. Delivering groceries proved to be quite *laborious*. Kim found himself carrying heavy bags up several flights of steps in four-story apartment buildings.
   (A) exciting   (B) difficult and demanding
   (C) relaxing and refreshing   (D) interesting and informative

Words

apprentice

aptitude

drudgery

journeyman

laborious

lackey

laggard

menial

nepotism

seniority

1. _____

2. _____

3. _____

4. _____

5. _____

6. Ms. Santos did not want some *lackey* for her assistant. She   6. _____
preferred an independent thinker, not someone who always
agreed with her.
(A) humble servant   (B) troublemaker
(C) lazy or untrustworthy   (D) lawbreaker
worker

7. If the production line is to work properly, everyone must do his or   7. _____
her job promptly. One *laggard* will reduce output considerably.
(A) dishonest worker   (B) slow worker
(C) careless worker   (D) beginner or novice

8. Without a high school diploma, Freida was able to get only *menial*   8. _____
jobs running errands and mowing lawns.
(A) satisfying   (B) difficult to learn
(C) simple and low-paying   (D) highly desirable

9. After the new manager hired his wife for a high-paying job and   9. _____
promoted his nephew over more deserving workers, the union
complained. Such *nepotism* had no place in the modern office.
(A) ability to think quickly   (B) willingness to compromise
(C) ability to make smart   (D) favoritism toward relatives
business decisions

10. When layoffs began, those with the shortest amount of time on the   10. _____
job were let go first. Those with more *seniority* had more job security.
(A) length of service in a job   (B) age
(C) sales and marketing ability   (D) outdated skills

Applying Meaning

Follow the directions below to write a sentence using a vocabulary word.

1. Write a sentence about a job you dislike. Use the word *menial* in your sentence.

_____

_____

_____

2. Use the word *aptitude* in a sentence about a special skill you have.

_____

_____

_____

3. Use *journeyman* in a sentence about a worker at a construction site.

_____

_____

_____

4. Write a sentence about a job someone had to perform. Use the word *laborious* in your sentence.

_____

_____

_____

5. Use the word *apprentice* in a sentence about a company that builds new homes.

_____

_____

_____

6. Use the word *drudgery* in a sentence about a boring job.

_____

_____

_____

Decide which word in parentheses best completes the sentence. Then write the sentence, adding the missing word.

7. Our company treats workers fairly. All raises and promotions will be based on merit and _____ . (nepotism; seniority)

_____

_____

_____

8. Because she was so eager to please her boss, June became a hopeless _____ . (laggard; lackey)

_____

_____

_____

9. The sportswriter was a _____ whose copy was always late. (journeyman; laggard)

_____

_____

_____

10. Although her nephew was clearly the most qualified worker, Ms. Cortez was accused of _____ when she promoted him. (nepotism; seniority)

_____

_____

_____

Our Living Language

The names for parts of the human body are often used in a figurative way to describe things around us. We refer to the *shoulder* of the road and the *eye* of a storm.

Make a List: Use each of the following names for parts of the body in a phrase describing something else.

finger	arm	nose
elbow	neck	lip

Name _____

The root *-gen-* found in a number of English words comes from two closely related Latin words. One is the Latin verb *gignere* meaning "to produce." The other is the word *genus*, meaning "kind" or "type" as in "I like that kind of pizza." This Latin word probably had its origins in the Greek word *genos*, meaning "race" or "kind." The Latin word for "death" is *mort*. English words with this root nearly always have something to do with death.

Root	Meaning	English Word
-gen-	to produce	regenerate
-gen-	kind, type, race	genetic
-mort-	death	mortality

A vocabulary word appears in italics in each sentence or short passage below. Find the root in each vocabulary word and choose the letter for the correct definition. Write the letter of your choice on the answer line.

Words

generation
genetic
genial
gentry
germinate
immortal
mortality
mortician
postmortem
regenerate

1. My *generation* takes space travel and computers for granted. My grandparents, however, are amazed by such things.
   (A) group of children   (B) people born about the same time
   (C) foreign invaders   (D) group of scientists

1. _____

2. It is easy to pick out members of my family. Our red hair, green eyes, and other *genetic* features make us stand out in almost any crowd.
   (A) beautiful   (B) remarkable
   (C) foolish   (D) inherited

2. _____

3. You could not ask for a more *genial* hostess than Fran. Her sincere smile and concern for her guests makes everyone feel comfortable.
   (A) intelligent   (B) cheerful and friendly
   (C) exhausted   (D) quiet

3. _____

4. Unlike Lincoln, Washington and Jefferson were members of the *gentry*. They came from educated families and owned large areas of land.
   (A) people of high standing   (B) religious fanatics
   (C) royalty   (D) leaders of a political party

4. _____

5. The rich earth and gentle rain caused the tulips to *germinate* early this year. We noticed their green stems poking up through the ground by the end of March.
   (A) die   (B) become infected
   (C) begin to grow   (D) take on bright colors

5. _____

6. Few who hear them will ever forget Martin Luther King's *immortal*
   words, "I have a dream." Even after this generation is gone, King's
   words will be quoted again and again.
   (A) illegal   (B) confusing
   (C) living on forever   (D) forgotten

6. _____

7. Young people often feel they will live forever, so the death of
   someone close to them is a shock. It reminds them of their own
   mortality.
   (A) certainty of death   (B) code of behavior
   (C) foolishness   (D) memory

7. _____

8. Jan's family owns and operates a very successful funeral service.
   Her parents want her to become a *mortician* and take over the
   business.
   (A) type of wall covering   (B) someone with limited abilities
   (C) type of doctor   (D) a funeral director or undertaker

8. _____

9. A lengthy *postmortem* indicated that the puzzling deaths of two
   patients were both the results of heart attacks.
   (A) someone in charge of   (B) examination of a body to
       preparing reports   decide the cause of death
   (C) former member of a royal (D) part of a hospital where dying
       family   patients are kept

9. _____

10. Although his team was far behind, the coach hoped his half-time
    speech would *regenerate* the players' enthusiasm.
    (A) give new life to   (B) put an end to
    (C) reduce or remove   (D) explain

10. _____

Applying Meaning

Read each sentence below. Write "correct" on the answer line if the vocabulary word has been used correctly or "incorrect" if it has been used incorrectly.

1. In some cultures it is not considered proper for women to appear in public alone. Such behavior is considered *immortal*.

2. Good food, fair prices, and a *genial* wait staff are all necessary to make a restaurant successful.

3. After the flood, the authorities asked all residents to *germinate* their water before drinking it.

4. The speaker asked all of us to think of how pollution affects the world we leave for the next *generation*.

5. Jeff's grandfather, a famous *mortician*, gave a great performance.

6. Before the death could be ruled a murder, the police and the prosecutor needed the results of the *postmortem*.

1. _____

2. _____

3. _____

4. _____

5. _____

6. _____

For each word used incorrectly, write a sentence using the word properly.

_____

_____

_____

_____

_____

_____

_____

_____

_____

Follow the directions below to write a sentence using a vocabulary word.

7. Use any form of the word *generate* to describe a change you or someone else decides to make in his or her life.

_____

_____

_____

8. Use the word *genetic* in a sentence about something affecting a family.

_____

_____

_____

9. Write something a religious leader might tell his followers. Use the word *mortality*.

_____

_____

_____

10. Use the word *gentry* to describe a group of people in history or in your community.

_____

_____

_____

Test-Taking Strategies

Some standardized tests ask you to choose the best word or words to complete a sentence. Sometimes two or more words will fit the sentence. In these cases it is important to choose the best answer. This is usually the answer that is more exact.

Practice: Choose the word or set of words that, when used in the sentence, best fits the meaning of the sentence as a whole.

1. Faced with certain execution, Prince John decided to _____ his claim to the throne.
   (A) prove   (B) deny
   (C) relinquish   (D) renew

2. The high waves made me feel somewhat _____ about climbing into the boat and rowing across the lake.
   (A) hesitant   (B) puzzled
   (C) shy   (D) firm

Name _____

How well do you remember the words you studied in Lessons 4 through 6? Take the following test covering the words from the last three lessons.

Part 1 Antonyms

Each question below includes a word in capital letters, followed by four words or phrases. Choose the word or phrase that is most nearly <u>opposite</u> in meaning to the word in capital letters. Consider all choices before deciding on your answer. Write the letter for your answer on the line provided.

Sample

S. SLOW	(A) lazy (C) fast	(B) simple (D) common	S. _____C_____
1. TEMPORARY	(A) logical (C) everlasting	(B) punctual (D) cold	1. _____
2. DRUDGERY	(A) easy and fun (C) useless	(B) without pay (D) boredom	2. _____
3. INSIGNIFICANT	(A) written down (C) characteristic	(B) ancient (D) meaningful	3. _____
4. TOLERATE	(A) oppose (C) line up	(B) consider (D) grow	4. _____
5. MORTALITY	(A) house payment (C) eternal life	(B) coverage (D) signal	5. _____
6. APPRENTICE	(A) teacher (C) woodworker	(B) cook (D) student	6. _____
7. IMMORTAL	(A) short-lived (C) long	(B) powerful (D) religious	7. _____
8. FLEXIBLE	(A) strong (C) useful	(B) rigid (D) tired	8. _____
9. GENIAL	(A) magical (C) charming	(B) dignified (D) unfriendly	9. _____
10. REGENERATE	(A) refuse (C) cool	(B) create (D) destroy	10. _____

11. LABORIOUS   (A) supportive   (B) easy   11. _____
(C) silly   (D) wild

12. EXPANSION   (A) without cause   (B) forever   12. _____
(C) shrinkage   (D) lost

13. LAGGARD   (A) boaster   (B) hard worker   13. _____
(C) modesty   (D) enemy

14. MENIAL   (A) kind   (B) elevated   14. _____
(C) dry   (D) helpful

15. PREPONDERANCE   (A) lesser part   (B) costly goods   15. _____
(C) afterthought   (D) invisible part

Part 2 Matching Words and Meaning

Match the definition in Column B with the word in Column A. Write the letter of the correct definition on the line provided.

Column A

16. nepotism
17. germinate
18. dominate
19. automation
20. aptitude
21. generation
22. postmortem
23. journeyman
24. mortician
25. seniority

Column B

a. funeral director
b. natural ability
c. control
d. examination after death
e. favor shown to relatives
f. experienced worker
g. people born about the same time
h. to begin to grow
i. use of machines
j. being older or having more time on a job

16. _____
17. _____
18. _____
19. _____
20. _____
21. _____
22. _____
23. _____
24. _____
25. _____

Name _____

Tornadoes

Filled with exciting special effects, the 1996 movie *Twister* attempted to show the awesome force of tornadoes. It also pretended to show how weather researchers study tornadoes. In the movie, fictional meteorologists actually "chased" tornadoes. Movie fans all over the
5   world responded to the film with enthusiastic **accolades**. However, the film also **garnered** severe criticism from educators and meteorologists. Its fictional scientists did not act wisely or even realistically. In fact, they **rashly** put themselves in the paths of raging tornadoes over and over again.
10   Whirling with tremendous **fury**, at speeds of up to 500 miles per hour, tornadoes are nature's most **perilous** storms. In minutes, a tornado can **devastate** everything in its path. When a tornado touched down in Jarrell, Texas, in 1997, the destruction was **extensive.** A housing development was destroyed, twenty-nine
15   people were killed, and hundreds were left homeless.
        Shaped like a tall, thin funnel, a tornado's path is quite narrow and unpredictable. If a tornado strikes a neighborhood, for example, it might destroy houses on one side of the street and leave those on the other side of the street untouched. Although terribly destructive,
20   tornadoes are quite **transitory**; most last only a few minutes.
        Tornadoes can occur at any time of year and have been spotted in all regions of the United States. However, the most severe tornadoes occur **primarily** in the spring in the Midwest and Texas. Masses of hot, dry air exist in the atmosphere above the southwestern plateau
25   of New Mexico. When these winds move eastward, they meet the humid, moist air of the Mississippi Valley and the Gulf of Mexico. The mixture of these air masses often leads to a violent thunderstorm, which can develop into a tornado.
        Tornadoes form so rapidly that there is little warning. However,
30   Dr. Joshua Wurman and his **colleagues** at the University of Oklahoma and the National Severe Storms Laboratory recently made a breakthrough in tornado research. They have developed a truck-mounted radar device that measures the wind speeds and the upward and downward drafts within a tornado's funnel. "With
35   greater knowledge, we may one day be able to lengthen warning times from, say, five minutes to fifteen minutes," Dr. Wurman stated. "That margin could save lives by giving people a little more time to run to storm cellars."

Words

accolade

colleague

devastate

extensive

fury

garner

perilous

primarily

rashly

transitory

Each word in this lesson's word list appears in dark type in the selection you just read. Think about how the vocabulary word is used in the selection. Then write the letter for the best answer to each question.

1. Which word or words could best replace *accolades* in line 5?   1. _____
   (A) words of criticism   (B) words of praise
   (C) questions   (D) requests

2. Which word or words could best replace *garnered* in line 6?   2. _____
   (A) gave   (B) received or earned
   (C) was grateful for   (D) looked forward to

3. Someone who acts *rashly* (line 8) is _____.   3. _____
   (A) cautious and brave   (B) scientific and professional
   (C) wise   (D) reckless

4. Which word or words could best replace *fury* in line 10?   4. _____
   (A) chill factors   (B) duration
   (C) violent force   (D) moisture

5. Another word for *perilous* (line 11) is _____.   5. _____
   (A) dangerous   (B) curious
   (C) gentle   (D) rare

6. Which word could best replace *devastate* in line 12?   6. _____
   (A) control   (B) rearrange
   (C) affect   (D) destroy

7. Which word or words could best replace *extensive* in line 14?   7. _____
   (A) small   (B) large and widespread
   (C) moderate   (D) interesting

8. A *transitory* (line 20) tornado is _____.   8. _____
   (A) violent   (B) swirling
   (C) brief   (D) colorful

9. The word *primarily* in line 23 means _____.   9. _____
   (A) rarely   (B) most often
   (C) sometimes   (D) never

10. Which word or words could best replace *colleagues* in line 30?   10. _____
    (A) ancestors   (B) family members
    (C) partners   (D) secretaries

Applying Meaning

Follow the directions below to write a sentence using a vocabulary word.

1. Describe the foods you eat for breakfast. Use the word *primarily*.

   _____

   _____

   _____

2. Write a sentence about two people. Use the word *colleagues*.

   _____

   _____

   _____

3. Describe an audience's response to a performance by a singer. Use the word *accolades*.

   _____

   _____

   _____

4. Give a reason for not doing something. Use the word *perilous*.

   _____

   _____

   _____

5. Use any form of the word *devastate* in a sentence about something that was reported in the news.

   _____

   _____

   _____

Read each sentence below. Write "correct" on the answer line if the vocabulary word has been used correctly or "incorrect" if it has been used incorrectly.

6. Holding her baby gently, Mrs. Peters sang a lullaby with *fury*.

6. _____

7. Perhaps spring flowers are appreciated more because they are so *transitory*.

7. _____

8. Helen wanted to save her money, so she spent it very *rashly*.

8. _____

9. Before buying the house, Jorge did *extensive* research on the area, its schools, and its taxes.

9. _____

10. Her excellent performance *garnered* hearty applause from the audience.

10. _____

For each word used incorrectly, write a sentence using the word properly.

_____

_____

_____

_____

_____

_____

_____

_____

_____

_____

Mastering Meaning

Do you think that it is proper for moviemakers to change certain facts to make a more exciting movie? In the movie *Twister*, the heroes studied tornadoes by chasing them. Scientists do not study tornadoes this way. This is not only inaccurate; it is dangerous. Write an essay stating your opinion of this practice. Use some of the words you studied in this lesson.

Lesson 8 Part A

Name _____

Animals have always been important to humans as food, as helpers, and as symbols. For instance, snails are associated with slowness and foxes with intelligence. In this lesson, you will learn ten animal words that are used to describe people. The qualities these animals have—or are thought to have—are often associated with people.

Unlocking Meaning

Words
badger
beastly
bovine
dogged
lame duck
lionize
mammoth
scapegoat
sheepish
sluggish

Read the sentences or short passages below. Write the letter for the correct definition of the italicized vocabulary word.

1. The witness has answered that question three times. If you continue to *badger* her into changing her answer, the jury may begin to feel sorry for her.
   (A) flatter   (B) bully
   (C) joke with   (D) ignore

2. Because of the *beastly* weather, we did not expect a large crowd at the parade. We were surprised that so many people showed up.
   (A) pleasant   (B) dark
   (C) dry   (D) disagreeable

1. _____

3. He spent the summer watching television, eating snacks, and sleeping. Thanks to this *bovine* behavior, he gained twenty pounds.
   (A) dull or slow   (B) active
   (C) peaceful   (D) exciting

2. _____

4. My cousin is not someone who gives up easily. Sometimes I find his *dogged* determination annoying, but he always finishes everything he starts.
   (A) friendly   (B) silly
   (C) stubborn   (D) angry

3. _____

4. _____

5. Although she was defeated in the last election, Senator Walker still must complete her term. However, like most *lame duck* senators, she has lost much of her power.
   (A) good swimmers   (B) defeated or helpless
   (C) speechless   (D) effective

5. _____

6. Many people *lionize* athletes and actors while ignoring scientists and teachers. Yet scientists and teachers have a more lasting impact on our lives.

(A) rule over   (B) make fun of

(C) do not notice   (D) treat as important

6. _____

7. I had no room for dessert after finishing such a *mammoth* sandwich.

(A) huge   (B) dark

(C) vegetarian   (D) old-fashioned

7. _____

8. Although several people actually committed the crime, one person was made the *scapegoat*. He was sent to jail while the others were freed.

(A) lucky person   (B) one blamed for the mistakes of others

(C) winner of an award   (D) defender of animals

8. _____

9. Elena asked everyone to help her find her glasses. She felt quite *sheepish* when someone pointed out that they were on top of her head.

(A) slow   (B) embarrassed

(C) joyful   (D) loud

9. _____

10. Yesterday I swept and vacuumed the house, but today's heat makes me too *sluggish* to do anything active.

(A) clean and clear   (B) sly

(C) slightly damp   (D) drained of energy

10. _____

Applying Meaning

Each question below contains at least one vocabulary word from this lesson. Answer each question "yes" or "no" in the space provided.

1. If you needed to be rescued from a narrow cliff, would you want your rescuers to make *dogged* efforts to reach you?

1. _____

2. When giving a speech, would you enjoy being *badgered* with interruptions?

2. _____

3. Would you enjoy being made the *scapegoat* for a class prank?

3. _____

4. Do newspapers frequently *lionize* successful local athletes?

4. _____

5. If you had a *beastly* vacation at a theme park, would you want to visit it again next year?

5. _____

For each question you answered "no," write a sentence explaining your reason.

_____

_____

_____

_____

_____

_____

_____

_____

_____

_____

Read each sentence or short passage below. Write "correct" on the answer line if the vocabulary word has been used correctly or "incorrect" if it has been used incorrectly.

6. I awoke filled with confidence. I felt so *sluggish* that I was sure I would win the race.

6. _____

7. Only one person can fit inside this *mammoth* tent.

7. _____

8. Marge plays tennis and baseball every chance she gets, but her brother just watches her with a *bovine* stare on his face.

8. _____

9. After announcing his plan to quit his job, Sam was treated like a *lame duck*. He was given no important assignments, and few people spoke to him.

9. _____

10. No one had accused her of eating the leftover pizza, but her
    sheepish grin suggested she was guilty.

    10. _____

For each word used incorrectly, write a sentence using the word properly.

_____

_____

_____

_____

_____

_____

_____

_____

_____

Cultural Literacy Note

Dog in the Manger

One of Aesop's fables tells the story of a farmer who owned an ox and a dog. The dog liked to sleep in the manger, a box that held the ox's hay. One day the tired and hungry ox returned from a day of hard work and wanted nothing more than a few mouthfuls of sweet hay. The dog was not happy to be disturbed. When the ox stuck its head into the manger, the dog barked and snapped furiously.

The tired ox complained to its master. "The dog is truly impossible! It cannot eat the hay, but it keeps me from eating any!" Because of this popular story, "a dog in the manger" has referred to someone who spoils things for others, even though the spoiler can receive no benefit from it.

Write a Paragraph: Describe a situation in which someone acts like a dog in the manger. It might be a situation at school or at home. It might involve a real or imaginary person.

Name _____

The prefix *hyper-* comes from the Greek word *huper,* meaning "over," "above," or "beyond." The prefix *hypo-* comes from the Greek word *hupo,* meaning "under," "beneath," or "below." In a word like *hyperactive,* it is easy to add the meaning of the prefix to the base word and unlock the meaning of the word. However, when these prefixes are added to a root, the meaning may not be as clear.

Prefix	Meaning	English Word
hyper-	over, above, beyond	hyperactive
hypo-	under, beneath, below	hypodermic

Words

hyperactive

hyperbole

hyperextension

hypersonic

hypertension

hypochondriac

hypocrisy

hypodermic

hypotenuse

hypothetical

Unlocking Meaning

Read the sentences or short passages below. Write the letter for the correct definition of the italicized word.

1. The restaurant was full of *hyperactive* children running around the tables, crawling under chairs, and driving the waitresses crazy.
   (A) overly active   (B) quiet
   (C) lovable   (D) loud

   1. _____

2. Saying his books weigh a ton is just another example of Ed's use of *hyperbole.* Don't take him seriously.
   (A) charm   (B) deceit
   (C) humor   (D) exaggeration

   2. _____

3. When Joan pulled Jim down by his arm she caused a painful *hyperextension* of his shoulder.
   (A) examination   (B) rotation
   (C) break in the bone   (D) stretching a body part

   3. _____

4. As it returns to Earth the space shuttle reaches *hypersonic* speeds.
   (A) easily measured   (B) many times the speed of sound
   (C) dangerous   (D) impossible to record

   4. _____

5. When my blood pressure rose to alarming levels, the doctor prescribed some medication to control the *hypertension.*
   (A) type of airplane   (B) loss of energy
   (C) high blood pressure (D) expenses

   5. _____

6. A lifetime *hypochondriac*, my aunt Nell sees her doctor at least twice a week and always complains about her imaginary aches and pains.

(A) a person concerned about his or her health

(B) a person studying to be a doctor

(C) someone often convinced he or she is ill

(D) a close relative

6. _____

7. Campaigning for animal rights while eating a hamburger seems to me the height of *hypocrisy*.

(A) compassion

(B) expressing beliefs one does not hold

(C) free speech

(D) honor and bravery

7. _____

8. The immunization program required children to get a *hypodermic* injection.

(A) beneath the skin

(B) painful

(C) useless

(D) expensive

8. _____

9. Today we learned the formula for calculating the length of the *hypotenuse* when the length of the other two sides is known.

(A) African water animal

(B) unproved theory

(C) longest side of a right triangle

(D) source of water

9. _____

10. June used the *hypothetical* case of a person yelling "Fire!" in a crowded theater to prove that free speech is not always protected.

(A) an example used for the sake of argument

(B) far-fetched

(C) confusing

(D) too simple to be usable

10. _____

Name _____

Applying Meaning

Each question below contains at least one vocabulary word from this lesson. Answer each question "yes" or "no" in the space provided.

1. Does a measles shot require a *hypodermic* injection?

2. Would it be wise to take several *hyperactive* children into a glass and china store?

3. Is a *hypotenuse* a large African water animal?

4. Might a healthy *hypochondriac* insist he or she has *hypertension*?

5. Is the longest side of a triangle called the *hyperbole*?

6. Would you vote for a candidate with a history of *hypocrisy*?

1. _____

2. _____

3. _____

4. _____

5. _____

6. _____

For each question you answered "no," write a sentence explaining your reason.

_____

_____

_____

_____

_____

_____

_____

_____

_____

_____

Decide which word in parentheses best completes the sentence. Then write the sentence, adding the missing word.

7. The teacher tried to explain how a bill becomes a law with a _____ example. (hypersonic; hypothetical)

_____

_____

_____

8. Her claim of being the fastest runner in the state was dismissed as _____ by most of her competitors. (hyperbole; hyperextension)

_____

_____

_____

9. The equipment available in the laboratory was unable to measure such _____ speeds. (hyperactive; hypersonic)

_____

_____

_____

10. The team trainer said the _____ the quarterback suffered would keep him on the bench for three weeks. (hyperextension; hyperbole)

_____

_____

_____

Bonus Word

hype

One word that has worked its way into the English language is *hype*. It no doubt also comes from the Greek word *huper* and the English prefix *hyper-*. Although some dictionaries still classify the word as slang, others accept it as standard English because it fulfills the need to identify a certain element of modern living.

Write a Definition: Review the meaning of the Greek word *huper* and the English prefix *hyper-*. Then study how the word *hype* is used in the sentences below. Write a dictionary definition for this recently coined word.

There was a great deal of hype surrounding this year's Super Bowl.

All the magazine stories and television interviews are just so much hype for the new movie.

Name _____

How well do you remember the words you studied in Lessons 7 through 9? Take the following test covering the words from the last three lessons.

Part 1 Choose the Correct Meaning

Each question below includes a word in capital letters, followed by four words or phrases. Choose the word or phrase that is <u>closest</u> in meaning to the word in capital letters. Write the letter for your answer on the line provided.

Sample

S. FINISH	(A) enjoy	(B) complete	S. ____B____
	(C) destroy	(D) enlarge	

1. PRIMARILY   (A) seasonally   (B) rarely   1. _____
       (C) mostly   (D) singularly

2. BADGER   (A) annoy   (B) question   2. _____
       (C) describe   (D) praise

3. PERILOUS   (A) dangerous   (B) valuable   3. _____
       (C) small   (D) safe

4. HYPERBOLE   (A) type of triangle   (B) sickness   4. _____
       (C) flattery   (D) exaggeration

5. COLLEAGUE   (A) school   (B) coworker   5. _____
       (C) doctor   (D) gardener

6. BEASTLY   (A) terrible   (B) beautiful   6. _____
       (C) strange   (D) musical

7. EXTENSIVE   (A) colorful   (B) permanent   7. _____
       (C) forgotten   (D) widespread

8. SHEEPISH   (A) embarrassed   (B) soft   8. _____
       (C) loyal   (D) adorable

9. FURY   (A) happiness   (B) windiness   9. _____
       (C) anger   (D) uncertainty

10. HYPOCRISY   (A) success   (B) dishonesty   10. _____
       (C) cruelty   (D) trickery

11. TRANSITORY   (A) changeable   (B) simple   11. _____
                 (C) short-lived   (D) miniature

12. DEVASTATE   (A) enlarge   (B) rebuild   12. _____
                 (C) grow   (D) destroy

13. MAMMOTH   (A) large   (B) monthly   13. _____
                 (C) poisonous   (D) motherly

14. GARNER   (A) decorate   (B) condemn   14. _____
                 (C) earn   (D) release

15. LAME DUCK   (A) fast   (B) powerless   15. _____
                 (C) effortless   (D) small

Part 2 Matching Words and Meanings

Match the definition in Column B with the word in Column A. Write the letter of the correct definition on the line provided.

Column A	Column B	
16. hypothetical	a. to treat as important	16. _____
17. hypertension	b. tired	17. _____
18. lionize	c. one who worries excessively about health	18. _____
19. sluggish	d. stubborn	19. _____
20. dogged	e. one who is blamed for the crimes of others	20. _____
21. hypotenuse	f. overly energetic	21. _____
22. scapegoat	g. based on a theory	22. _____
23. hypodermic	h. the longest side of a right triangle	23. _____
24. hypochondriac	i. under the skin	24. _____
25. hyperactive	j. high blood pressure	25. _____

Name _____

The Story of Icarus and Daedalus

King Minos was the son of Zeus, the most important of the Greek gods. Minos, who ruled the island of Crete, was a **fickle** ruler. He might love his subjects one day and **despise** them the next. Daedalus and his son Icarus were the victims of the king's change-

5 able moods. Even though Daedalus had built the famous Labyrinth for King Minos, the king had Daedalus and his son imprisoned on an island. There Daedalus and Icarus spent their days watching seagulls float freely through the air. These birds gave Daedalus an idea for escaping his unjust **incarceration**.

10 Daedalus began to collect feathers and to form them into huge wings. Then he tied the feathers together with string and poured melted wax over them. As the wax cooled and hardened, it formed a **cohesive** glue. Next Daedalus fastened the wings to his shoulders and began to **cleave** the air by flapping his new wings back and

15 forth. Slowly he began to rise from the ground and glide over his island prison.

When he floated back to earth, Daedalus immediately began to **mold** a set of wings for his son. Soon father and son were prepared to make their escape, but before taking to the air, Daedalus gave

20 Icarus some final advice. "Remember, do not soar too high. The heat of the sun will melt the wax, and your wings will fall apart." Icarus was young, however, and he **disdained** all advice from his elders. Once he was in the air, the joy he felt over his escape and the power of his youth **prompted** him to sail higher and higher into the air.

25 Nothing could **quench** his desire to reach the heavens.

The higher he flew, the warmer the air became. Gradually the wings grew limp, and then they began to **disintegrate**. Feathers fluttered to the ground. Icarus tried flapping his wings harder and harder, but it was of no use. He fell headlong into the sea. Hearing

30 his son's cries, Daedalus began searching for him, but all he found were hundreds of feathers floating on the sea. He knew Icarus had drowned. So is it ever with youth who try to soar too high and too fast on fragile wings.

Words
cleave
cohesive
despise
disdain
disintegrate
fickle
incarceration
mold
prompt
quench

Unlocking Meaning

Each word in this lesson's word list appears in dark type in the selection you just read. Think about how the vocabulary word is used in the selection, then write the letter for the best answer to each question.

1. A *fickle* (line 2) ruler _____.
   (A) is the son of a powerful god   (B) is just and fair
   (C) exists only in the   (D) frequently changes his or
       imagination   her mind.

1. _____

2. If you *despise* (line 3) someone, you _____.
   (A) have a strong dislike for   (B) watch the person secretly
       that person
   (C) admire the person   (D) have power over that person

2. _____

3. Another word for *incarceration* (line 9) is _____.
   (A) admiration   (B) imprisonment
   (C) confusion   (D) kingdom

3. _____

4. If something is *cohesive*, (line 13) it _____.
   (A) is difficult to understand   (B) sticks together
   (C) cannot be found   (D) falls apart easily

4. _____

5. If you *cleave* (line 14) the air, you _____.
   (A) cause it to become dirty   (B) examine it closely
   (C) divide or split it   (D) meet it face to face

5. _____

6. To *mold* (line 18) is to _____.
   (A) give shape to   (B) force
   (C) forecast   (D) destroy

6. _____

7. If you *disdain* (line 22) someone's advice, you _____.
   (A) follow it   (B) listen to it carefully
   (C) reject it rudely   (D) share it with others

7. _____

8. In line 24, *prompted* means _____.
   (A) frightened   (B) tricked
   (C) warned   (D) encouraged

8. _____

9. Another word for *quench* (line 25) is _____.
   (A) heighten   (B) expand
   (C) deliver   (D) satisfy

9. _____

10. If something *disintegrates*, (line 27) it _____.
    (A) comes together   (B) falls apart
    (C) rises into the air   (D) turns over

10. _____

Applying Meaning

Decide which word in parentheses best completes the sentence.
Then write the sentence, adding the missing word.

1. A good leader cannot afford to be _____ in a time of crisis.
   (cohesive; fickle)

   _____

   _____

   _____

2. The mayor had come to _____ the newspaper's constant criticism of
   his actions. (disdain; disintegrate)

   _____

   _____

   _____

3. The Civil War threatened to _____ the Union into separate nations.
   (cleave; mold)

   _____

   _____

   _____

4. The coach had many talented players, but it would take weeks to
   teach them to play as a _____ team. (cohesive; fickle)

   _____

   _____

   _____

5. Her father's sudden illness _____ Juanita to leave her job and rush
   to his bedside. (prompted; quenched)

   _____

   _____

   _____

Read each sentence below. Write "correct" on the answer line if the
vocabulary word has been used correctly or "incorrect" if it has been
used incorrectly.

6. After ten years of *incarceration*, the prisoner's conviction was   6. _____
   reversed and he was set free.

7. The city notified the abandoned building's owner that she would have to *mold* it.

7. _____

8. No matter how much we dislike the umpire's calls, our coach will not allow us to *disintegrate* those decisions.

8. _____

9. American patriots had admired the skill and bravery of Benedict Arnold, but after Arnold betrayed his country, they came to *despise* the man.

9. _____

10. The Mars space probe is an outstanding example of science's ongoing *quench* for knowledge.

10. _____

For each word used incorrectly, write a sentence using the word properly.

_____

_____

_____

_____

_____

_____

_____

_____

_____

_____

Mastering Meaning

Think about the last sentence in the story of Icarus and Daedalus: "So is it ever with youth who try to soar too high and too fast on fragile wings." Does this statement apply to young people today? What does it mean to soar too high and too fast? What are the fragile wings? Write a short essay agreeing or disagreeing with the statement. Use examples from your own experience to support your position. In your essay, use some of the words you studied in this lesson.

Vocabulary of Faith and Religion

Lesson 11 Part A

Name _____

Religion plays an important part in many people's lives. Whether or not you practice a particular religion, you will still read and hear many words that are related to faith and religion. Some of these words have more than one meaning. One definition may relate to something specific in the religion itself. The other meaning might be a more general term that is used in ordinary speech and writing.

Unlocking Meaning

Read the sentences or short passages below. Write the letter for the correct definition of the italicized vocabulary word.

1. The priest asked visitors to the *basilica* to dress in a way that showed respect for the members' religious beliefs.
   (A) form of transportation
   (B) type of church building
   (C) article of clothing
   (D) religious activity

2. Many members of the *clergy* wear special clothing when performing religious ceremonies.
   (A) people who build windows
   (B) people who sell things in stores
   (C) people accompanied by children
   (D) people authorized to conduct religious services

3. In this section of the library you will find the *Koran*, the Bible, and other religious books.
   (A) sacred writings of Islam
   (B) schedules for the week
   (C) window that opens with a crank
   (D) person who keeps records

4. Most stores and restaurants in Jewish neighborhoods offer a large assortment of *kosher* foods.
   (A) spoiled
   (B) exposed to strong light
   (C) meeting standards of Jewish dietary laws
   (D) necessary for good dental health

5. Front-row seats are reserved for religious officials. The rest are for the *laity*.
   (A) family from a foreign country
   (B) people who accept no religion
   (C) women in government
   (D) members of a religious group who are not officials of the group

Words

- basilica
- clergy
- Koran
- kosher
- laity
- mecca
- menorah
- mosque
- mullah
- sanctuary

1. _____

2. _____

3. _____

4. _____

5. _____

6. Florida has become a *mecca* for students on spring break. The crowds of sun worshipers grow every year.
   (A) source of difficulty
   (B) center of important activity or interest
   (C) classroom
   (D) prison

   6. _____

7. When the last candle in our *menorah* was lit, we all agreed that it was a beautiful and inspiring sight.
   (A) decorated eating tools
   (B) furniture covering made of fine cloth
   (C) candleholder used in Jewish worship
   (D) string of beads used by several religions

   7. _____

8. This time of year has many holidays. It seems as if every church, *mosque*, and synagogue is filled.
   (A) Muslim house of worship
   (B) religious song
   (C) container for jewelry
   (D) place where clothing is hung

   8. _____

9. In certain Middle Eastern countries, few question the word of a *mullah*. His wisdom is considered supreme.
   (A) place where people gather
   (B) special holidays
   (C) a religious teacher
   (D) people who raise money

   9. _____

10. Some of the most important events in my life took place inside this church's *sanctuary*.
    (A) collection of books
    (B) sacred chamber or room; safe place
    (C) storage area
    (D) statue of an important person

    10. _____

Applying Meaning

Decide which word in parentheses best completes the sentence. Then write the sentence, adding the missing word.

1. In many churches, the _____ receive not only a salary, but also a home and a car for their service to the people. (clergy; laity)

   _____

   _____

   _____

2. Inside the _____ was a small courtyard. In the center of this stood a lovely fountain. (mullah; mosque)

   _____

   _____

   _____

3. In many homes, it is the mother who lights the candles in the _____. (menorah; mecca)

   _____

   _____

   _____

4. Prior to her wedding, Maria had been in the _____ only one other time, at her baptism. (sanctuary; Koran)

   _____

   _____

   _____

5. The _____ had been built by local workers using stones from a nearby quarry. (basilica; menorah)

   _____

   _____

   _____

Each question below contains at least one vocabulary word from this lesson. Answer each question "yes" or "no" in the space provided.

6. Would you expect to find writing in the *Koran*?   6. _____

7. Would you expect to find ham on the menu in a *kosher* restaurant?   7. _____

8. Is a holy city a *mecca* for devout members of a religion?   8. _____

9. Would a tired traveler try to get some rest and relaxation at a *laity*?   9. _____

10. Would a *mullah* spend a great deal of time studying sacred writings?   10. _____

For each question you answered "no," write a sentence explaining your reason.

_____

_____

_____

_____

_____

_____

_____

_____

Our Living Language

inferno

The word *inferno*, meaning "a hell-like place of great suffering," is actually the Italian word for *hell*. It comes from the Latin *infernus*, which means "underground or lower place." The Italian poet Dante Alighieri used the word to describe his vision of hell in his epic poem, *The Divine Comedy*. The adjective *infernal*, meaning "awful" comes from this word.

Cooperative Learning: Obtain an illustrated copy of Dante's *The Divine Comedy.* How does the illustration of hell compare to the picture of hell as you imagine it?

Name _____

When the meaning of a word has something to do with a number, it frequently includes a prefix from Latin or Greek. The Latin word for one is *unus*. The prefix *uni-,* meaning "one," can be seen in words such as *unicycle*, which means "a one-wheeled vehicle." Similarly, *bi-* carries the meaning "two," and *tri-* has the meaning "three."

Prefix or Word Part	Meaning	English Word
uni-	one	unilateral
bi-	two; twice	bicentennial
tri-	three	tripod

Words

ambidextrous

ambivalent

bicentennial

bilingual

trilogy

tripod

triumvirate

unification

unilateral

unique

Unlocking Meaning

Write the vocabulary word that fits each clue below. Then say the word and write a short definition. Compare your definition with the one given in the dictionary at the back of the book.

1. Many classical Greek dramas consisted of three plays performed in sequence. The Greek word for this performance was *trilogia*.

   _____

   _____

   _____

2. On July 4, 1776, the United States adopted the Declaration of Independence. This anniversary was celebrated on July 4, 1976.

   _____

   _____

   _____

3. This word can be used to describe every word and every snowflake.

   _____

   _____

   _____

4. This word, which has something to do with government, contains a form of *vir*, the Latin word for "man."

_____

_____

_____

5. This word adds a number prefix to the Latin word *latus*, meaning "side."

_____

_____

_____

6. I cannot make up my mind between two feelings. I don't know whether I am happy or sad to be moving.

_____

_____

_____

7. This word describes someone who does things equally well with the left or right hand. It includes the Latin *dexter*, meaning "skillful."

_____

_____

_____

8. This noun is formed from the verb *unify*.

_____

_____

_____

9. This word combines the prefix meaning "two" with a form of the Latin word *lingua* meaning "language."

_____

_____

_____

10. The Greek word for "foot" is *pous*. You might use one of these to hold a camera steady when taking a picture.

_____

_____

_____

Applying Meaning

Decide which word in parentheses best completes the sentence. Then write the sentence, adding the missing word.

1. Although he is just a child, I feel quite _____ about forgiving Sam for losing my money. (ambivalent; unilateral)

   _____

   _____

   _____

2. His disregard for the rules of punctuation and capitalization make e. e. cummings _____ among poets. (ambidextrous; unique)

   _____

   _____

   _____

3. The general warned the country not to _____ destroy its weapons. This would leave us helpless if attacked. (ambivalently; unilaterally)

   _____

   _____

   _____

4. Power to govern the city was shared by a _____. (trilogy; triumvirate)

   _____

   _____

   _____

5. Most international flights have _____ pilots and flight attendants. (ambidextrous; bilingual)

   _____

   _____

   _____

Read each sentence below. Write "correct" on the answer line if the vocabulary word has been used correctly or "incorrect" if it has been used incorrectly.

6. Next semester I plan to take a course in advanced *trilogy*.　　6. _____

7. The *unification* of England and Scotland began under James I.　　7. _____

8. Founded in 1772, San Luis Obispo, California, celebrated its *bicentennial* in 1972.　　8. _____

9. Instead of clear answers, the politician offered only a few *ambidextrous* remarks.　　9. _____

10. The telescope was mounted on a *tripod* to hold it steady.　　10. _____

For each word used incorrectly, write a sentence using the word properly.

_____

_____

_____

_____

_____

_____

_____

_____

_____

Test-Taking Strategies

Some tests ask you to choose a word that means the opposite of a word in capital letters. These tests may try to trick you by including a synonym for the word as one of the answers. Remember that the test asks for the word that means the <u>opposite</u> of the first word.

Practice: On the line provided, write the letter for the word most nearly <u>opposite</u> in meaning to the word in capital letters.

1. TYPICAL　　(A) exceptional　　(B) commonplace　　1. _____
　　　　　　　　(C) attractive　　　(D) foolish

2. DILATE　　(A) add　　　　　　(B) expand　　　　2. _____
　　　　　　　　(C) withdraw　　　　(D) close

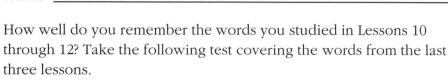

Assessment

Name _____

How well do you remember the words you studied in Lessons 10 through 12? Take the following test covering the words from the last three lessons.

Part 1 Choose the Correct Meaning

Each question below includes a word in capital letters, followed by four words or phrases. Choose the word or phrase that is <u>closest</u> in meaning to the word in capital letters. Write the letter for your answer on the line provided.

Sample

S. FINISH	(A) enjoy	(B) complete	S. ___**B**___
	(C) destroy	(D) enlarge	

1. BASILICA	(A) baseball diamond	(B) baptismal font	1. _____
	(C) priest's home	(D) place of worship	
2. UNIFICATION	(A) doing something alone	(B) joining together	2. _____
	(C) making a decision	(D) telling a tale	
3. MENORAH	(A) candleholder	(B) memory	3. _____
	(C) noble act	(D) stage light	
4. QUENCH	(A) extend	(B) satisfy	4. _____
	(C) justify	(D) relive	
5. INCARCERATION	(A) imprisonment	(B) rebirth	5. _____
	(C) repayment	(D) forgiven	
6. AMBIDEXTROUS	(A) skillful	(B) unclear	6. _____
	(C) skilled with either hand	(D) having high hopes	
7. BICENTENNIAL	(A) 200th year	(B) celebration	7. _____
	(C) antique	(D) patriotic	
8. DESPISE	(A) ignore	(B) respect	8. _____
	(C) enjoy	(D) hate	
9. UNIQUE	(A) matchless	(B) common	9. _____
	(C) simple	(D) interesting	
10. SANCTUARY	(A) religious music	(B) museum	10. _____
	(C) school	(D) holy place	

11. CLERGY   (A) secretaries   (B) church officials   11. _____
(C) choir members   (D) religious books

12. TRILOGY   (A) third part   (B) a three-part series   12. _____
(C) travel journal   (D) eating utensils

13. PROMPTED   (A) released   (B) encouraged   13. _____
(C) concealed   (D) delivered

14. MULLAH   (A) religious teacher   (B) farm animal   14. _____
(C) altar   (D) holy water

15. DISDAIN   (A) remove   (B) repeat   15. _____
(C) relive   (D) reject

Part 2 Matching Words and Meaning

Match the definition in Column B with the word in Column A.
Write the letter of the correct definition on the line provided.

Column A	**Column B**	
16. Koran	a. unified; held together	16. _____
17. ambivalent	b. in keeping with Jewish food laws	17. _____
18. mecca	c. able to speak two languages	18. _____
19. bilingual	d. sacred book of Islam	19. _____
20. cohesive	e. changeable	20. _____
21. disintegrate	f. a center for people with a particular interest	21. _____
22. laity	g. fall apart	22. _____
23. kosher	h. having conflicting thoughts	23. _____
24. fickle	i. members of a faith who are not officials	24. _____
25. mosque	j. Muslim house of worship	25. _____

Name _____

Giving Gifts

Today people travel farther and faster than at any time in history. While travel provides many opportunities to encounter new peoples and new cultures, it also has certain **pitfalls**. For example, many people attempt to show their goodwill toward others by offering
5 gifts. Although giving gifts to show friendship is an almost **universal** practice, gift-giving customs are not the same the world over.

Each country has its own set of rules. If you give a gift to someone from another country or culture, it is important to know the **etiquette** of that country. Otherwise, an act meant to show friend-
10 ship might have the **potential** to upset both the giver and the receiver. The wrong gift can insult or **antagonize** the person who receives it. It can damage a friendship rather than strengthen it.

Flowers are popular gifts for many occasions. Yet not all flowers are a good choice. Yellow daisies given to a sick friend would be
15 a serious **breach** of etiquette in certain areas. In some countries, yellow is a color you give an enemy, so giving yellow flowers to a friend would be quite **offensive**. White flowers, too, can be a poor choice. In China, white, not black, is the color of mourning, so white is linked with death.

20 You cannot **eliminate** gift-giving problems entirely simply by avoiding flowers. Other types of gifts can also be the source of embarrassment or even a direct insult. In some cultures, giving the gift of a clock could **alienate** the recipient rather then drawing him or her closer to you. This is because clocks or watches are seen
25 as reminders of death. Since clocks measure life, each tick brings a person closer to life's end. In several countries, people avoid giving anything sharp, such as knives, because such objects are seen as signs that the giver wishes to cut the friendship short.

With so many **cultural** differences, you may wonder how inter-
30 national businesspeople can stay out of trouble. How do they learn the unspoken rules of the countries they visit? Many international businesses now hire experts to advise them on such matters. These people explain all the important customs of a country. They know how to choose gifts that make everyone smile.

Words
alienate
antagonize
breach
cultural
eliminate
etiquette
offensive
pitfalls
potential
universal

Each word in this lesson's word list appears in dark type in the selection you just read. Think about how the vocabulary word is used in the selection, then write the letter for the best answer to each question.

1. Which word could best replace *pitfalls* in line 3?

   (A) tiny holes   (B) foods

   (C) traps   (D) jokes

1. _____

2. A *universal* practice (line 5) is one that takes place _____.

   (A) everywhere   (B) in underdeveloped countries

   (C) in Europe   (D) in school

2. _____

3. Which word or words could best replace *etiquette* in line 9?

   (A) location   (B) accepted behavior

   (C) traditional songs   (D) close friends

3. _____

4. Another word for *potential* (line 10) is _____.

   (A) authority   (B) desire

   (C) demand   (D) possibility

4. _____

5. Which word could best replace *antagonize* in line 11?

   (A) anger   (B) please

   (C) tire   (D) invite

5. _____

6. A *breach* (line 15) is a(n) _____.

   (A) act   (B) increase

   (C) violation   (D) reminder

6. _____

7. An *offensive* (line 17) gift _____.

   (A) upsets people   (B) is small

   (C) smells sweet   (D) is correct

7. _____

8. If you *eliminate* (line 20) a problem, you

   (A) make it worse   (B) notice it

   (C) experience it   (D) make it disappear

8. _____

9. If you *alienate* people (line 23), you _____.

   (A) make new friends   (B) invite them home

   (C) lose their friendship (D) photograph them

9. _____

10. *Cultural* (line 29) differences occur _____.

   (A) only among educated (B) among relatives in one family

       people

   (C) only in business   (D) between people with differing

                            beliefs and customs

10. _____

Applying Meaning

Follow the directions below to write a sentence using a vocabulary word.

1. Use any form of the word *universal* to describe a friendly act.

   _____

   _____

   _____

2. Use the word *offensive* in an apology.

   _____

   _____

   _____

3. Use any form of the word *eliminate* to tell someone to stop a certain action.

   _____

   _____

   _____

4. Use *etiquette* in a sentence about proper behavior.

   _____

   _____

   _____

5. Use any form of the word *potential* to describe how you avoided a problem.

   _____

   _____

   _____

Read each sentence or short passage below. Write "correct" on the answer line if the vocabulary word has been used correctly or "incorrect" if it has been used incorrectly.

6. Julie hoped her friend would *antagonize* her so they could become even closer friends.

   6. _____

7. Dishonesty in any form will *alienate* most people.

   7. _____

8. The police arrived when they learned that there had been a *breach* of the peace.

8. _____

9. Ada is just a *cultural* friend, but Chad and I are really close.

9. _____

10. If you're lucky, you will be able to experience some of the *pitfalls* of modern travel.

10. _____

For each word used incorrectly, write a sentence using the word properly.

_____

_____

_____

_____

_____

_____

_____

_____

_____

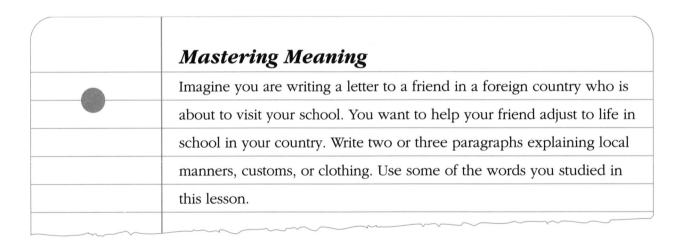

Mastering Meaning

Imagine you are writing a letter to a friend in a foreign country who is about to visit your school. You want to help your friend adjust to life in school in your country. Write two or three paragraphs explaining local manners, customs, or clothing. Use some of the words you studied in this lesson.

Confusing Words

Name _____

Words that look and sound alike but have different meanings can be the source of confusion for many writers. To avoid sending the wrong message and causing yourself great embarrassment, it is important to know the difference between similar words. In this lesson, you will learn five pairs of words that can be easily confused. Although they look and sound very much alike, these words have different meanings.

Words
biannual
biennial
human
humane
marital
martial
meddle
mettle
moral
morale

Unlocking Meaning

Read the sentences or short passages below. Write the letter for the correct definition of the italicized vocabulary word.

1. The Constitution calls for *biennial* elections to the House of Representatives.
   (A) occurring every two years   (B) occurring twice a year

2. The *biannual* meetings of the recreation committee are held in June and December.
   (A) occurring every two years   (B) occurring twice a year

3. The company replaced the answering machine with a live operator so customers could speak to a *human* being.
   (A) having the qualities of a   (B) kind, merciful, or
       living person   compassionate

4. Father Damien fought for the *humane* treatment of lepers at a time when they were treated as outcasts.
   (A) having the qualities of a   (B) kind, merciful, or
       living person   compassionate

5. The parade for the war hero began with a marching band playing rousing *martial* music.
   (A) related to marriage   (B) related to war and the military

6. On their golden anniversary, my parents repeated their *marital* vows.
   (A) related to marriage   (B) related to war and the military

1. _____

2. _____

3. _____

4. _____

5. _____

6. _____

7. President Monroe warned the European powers not to *meddle* in the affairs of the Americas.
   (A) to interfere with   (B) daring and courage

7. _____

8. The troops did well in training, but their *mettle* would be severely tested in actual combat.
   (A) to interfere with   (B) daring and courage

8. _____

9. The fable about the tortoise and the hare teaches the reader a *moral* about perseverance.
   (A) lesson or principle   (B) the state of one's spirits or mental state

9. _____

10. After the opposing team scored eight runs in the first inning, our *morale* reached its lowest point.
    (A) lesson or principle   (B) the state of one's spirits or mental state

10. _____

Applying Meaning

Decide which word in parentheses best completes the sentence. Then write the sentence, adding the missing word.

1. After reading the shocking reports of mistreatment, we demanded more _____ treatment of the prison population. (human; humane)

   _____

   _____

   _____

2. Property tax bills are sent to homeowners _____, usually in March and September. (biannually; biennially)

   _____

   _____

   _____

3. Although Huang thought Bruce was making a mistake, he chose not to _____ in another person's affairs. (meddle, mettle)

   _____

   _____

   _____

4. The _____ of the story was clear. (moral; morale)

   _____

   _____

   _____

5. In some cultures, it is a common _____ custom for the parents to choose spouses for their children. (marital; martial)

   _____

   _____

   _____

Read each sentence. Write "correct" on the answer line if the vocabulary word has been used correctly or "incorrect" if it has been used incorrectly.

6. Founded in 1630, Boston celebrated its *biennial* in 1830.   6. _____

7. It is not wise to *meddle* in your sister's business.   7. _____

8. The general raised the *morale* of the troops by telling them how proud he felt to be their commander.

8. _____

9. After months of intense study and practice in the *martial* arts, Sue was confident she could defend herself in any situation.

9. _____

10. The six-month trip to Mars will be a severe test of *human* endurance.

10. _____

For each word used incorrectly, write a sentence using the word properly.

_____

_____

_____

_____

_____

_____

_____

_____

_____

_____

The Dictionary

The dictionary provides information on the part of speech of each entry word. The example below shows how the word *moral* can be used as either an adjective or a noun.

mor·al (môr' əl or mŏr' əl) adj. 1. The judgment of an action as either good or bad: *Her decision is based on a moral principle.*

2. Teaching or expressing proper behavior. a moral act. —n.

A lesson taught by a story: *the moral of a fable.*

Check the Dictionary: Look up the following words in a classroom dictionary. Write the parts of speech given for each word. Then write an original sentence using the word as each part of speech.

| master | nurse | lance |
| knock | compound | exhaust |

Name _____

The prefixes *ante-* and *anti-* look and sound very much alike, but their meanings are quite different. The prefix *ante-* comes from the Latin word *ante*, meaning "before." If one event *antedates* another, it comes before it. The prefix *anti-* , meaning "opposite" or "against," comes from the Greek word *anti*. Someone who is *antismoking* is against smoking.

Prefix	Meaning	English Word
ante-	before	antedate
anti-	opposite, against	antisocial

Copyright © Glencoe/McGraw-Hill, a division of The McGraw-Hill Companies, Inc.

Words

antebellum

antecedent

antedate

anteroom

anticlimax

antidote

antipathy

antiseptic

antisocial

antitoxin

Unlocking Meaning

Write the vocabulary word that fits each clue below. Then say the word and write a short definition. Compare your definition with the one in the dictionary at the back of the book.

1. This word contains the Latin word *bellum* meaning "war." It describes the South before the Civil War.

   _____

   _____

   _____

2. Increasingly exciting events should build to a climax. This word describes what happens when things just come to an end, without a climax.

   _____

   _____

   _____

3. A toxin is a poison. If you swallow some, you'll need to take this.

   _____

   _____

   _____

4. This word contains the root *cedere*, meaning "to go." Every pronoun has one of these.

_____

_____

_____

5. This noun contains the root *pathos*, meaning "feeling." It is something you might have for an enemy.

_____

_____

_____

6. The Latin word *socius* means "companion." This word suggests that someone does not want or need a companion.

_____

_____

_____

7. A lobby or waiting room is a good example of this.

_____

_____

_____

8. The Greek word *septos* means "poisonous." You might use this to prevent a poisonous substance from entering your body.

_____

_____

_____

9. If you wrote a rent check on July 15 but dated it July 1, this word describes what you did.

_____

_____

_____

10. It could describe what laughter is to sadness, what food is to hunger, and what certain medication is for a snakebite.

_____

_____

_____

Applying Meaning

Decide which word in parentheses best completes the sentence. Then write the sentence, adding the missing word.

1. Potato crop failures in the 1840s were the _____ of Irish immigration to America in the 1850s. (antecedent; antidote)

   _____

   _____

   _____

2. Gwen had a strong _____ to air travel. (anticlimax; antipathy)

   _____

   _____

   _____

3. Jorge is not _____, but he had to work and couldn't spend the evening with his friends. (antiseptic; antisocial)

   _____

   _____

   _____

4. The antique dealer tried to _____ the historic document to make the buyer think it was much older. (antedate; antebellum)

   _____

   _____

   _____

5. A weekend alone in the woods was the perfect _____ for the hectic week Julio spent in the office. (anticlimax; antidote)

   _____

   _____

   _____

6. Because the risk of infection is so high, hospital rooms must always be kept in an _____ condition. (antecedent; antiseptic)

   _____

   _____

   _____

Follow the directions below to write a sentence using a vocabulary word.

7. Describe some aspect of life in the South before the Civil War.
   Use the word *antebellum*.

   _____

   _____

   _____

8. Use the word *anteroom* in a sentence about a public building such
   as a museum or courthouse.

   _____

   _____

   _____

9. Tell about a vacation you looked forward to. Use the word
   anticlimax.

   _____

   _____

   _____

10. Describe a life-threatening event or situation. Use the word
    antitoxin.

    _____

    _____

    _____

Our Living Language

The prefix *anti-* is one of the most flexible prefixes in the English language. It is easily added to existing words to form new words that most people will understand immediately. During the 1960s the words *antiwar* and *antiestablishment* emerged. More recently, *antiabortion* and *antidumping* have become common.

Cooperative Learning: Work with a partner to write a dictionary definition and sample sentence for each of the following words: antibusiness, antibusing, antifeminist, antigun, antinuclear, antipollution, antismog, antitank

Name _____

How well do you remember the words you studied in Lessons 13 through 15? Take the following test covering the words from the last three lessons.

Part 1 Antonyms

Each question below includes a word in capital letters, followed by four words or phrases. Choose the word or phrase that is most nearly <u>opposite</u> in meaning to the word in capital letters. Write the letter for your answer on the line provided.

Sample

S. SLOW	(A) lazy (C) fast	(B) simple (D) common	S. ___C___

1. UNIVERSAL	(A) distant (C) educated	(B) limited (D) weak	1. _____
2. HUMANE	(A) cruel (C) kind	(B) mechanical (D) intelligent	2. _____
3. ANTISEPTIC	(A) ancient (C) clean	(B) safe (D) filthy	3. _____
4. MARTIAL	(A) bright (C) earthly	(B) official (D) civilian	4. _____
5. ANTEDATE	(A) follow (C) lead	(B) court (D) accompany	5. _____
6. BREACH	(A) connection (C) provision	(B) division (D) break	6. _____
7. ANTIPATHY	(A) immortal (C) huge	(B) attraction (D) hatred	7. _____
8. OFFENSIVE	(A) insulting (C) harmless	(B) odorous (D) clever	8. _____
9. ANTISOCIAL	(A) rude (C) cute	(B) business-like (D) friendly	9. _____
10. PITFALLS	(A) resting places (C) dangers	(B) advantages (D) challenges	10. _____

11. ANTITOXIN   (A) warlike   (B) poison   11. _____

                      (C) type of leaf   (D) electric

12. ELIMINATE   (A) keep   (B) destroy   12. _____

                      (C) darken   (D) understand

13. ANTEBELLUM   (A) beautiful   (B) awkward   13. _____

                      (C) historic   (D) postwar

14. ALIENATE   (A) befriend   (B) explore   14. _____

                      (C) discharge   (D) renew

15. ANTAGONIZE   (A) protest   (B) identify   15. _____

                      (C) comfort   (D) apply heat

Part 2 Matching Words and Meanings

Match the definition in Column B with the word in Column A.
Write the letter of the correct definition on the line provided.

Column A	Column B	
16. meddle	a. related to customs and beliefs	16. _____
17. etiquette	b. daring and courage	17. _____
18. biennial	c. coming or happening before	18. _____
19. morale	d. possibility or probability	19. _____
20. antecedent	e. occurring twice a year	20. _____
21. cultural	f. lesson or principle	21. _____
22. mettle	g. rules of polite behavior	22. _____
23. moral	h. spirit or mental state	23. _____
24. potential	i. to interfere	24. _____
25. biannual	j. occurring once every two years	25. _____

Name _____

Autopsy

Regardless of one's beliefs about the spiritual life of the soul, the treatment of our earthly remains is a matter of considerable importance. In nearly all cultures, the **desecration** of a dead body, even the body of an enemy, is **abhorrent**. Extreme measures are taken
5 to recover the victims of mining disasters, plane crashes, and other accidents in order that their bodies may be properly buried. The cremated remains of loved ones are usually handled with great reverence. They have been lovingly scattered over the sea, housed in shrines, and even shot into space.
10   It is little surprise then that the idea of cutting apart and studying a dead body is charged with deep emotions. The thought of cutting into the human body was deeply **repugnant** to the early Chinese and Muslims. In the Middle Ages, many Western civilizations prohibited such human **dissection**. Even today, authorizing
15 an autopsy on the body of a loved one can be a heart-wrenching decision.
      It was not until the Renaissance that the dissection and study of corpses became an acceptable scientific practice. Only then was it possible to **differentiate** between the normal and abnormal
20 appearances of human organs and to begin to link certain **symptoms** of a disease with observable abnormalities.
      Until the nineteenth century, autopsies were limited to observations that could be made with the naked eye. The microscope made it possible to study the changes in the cells and link their **mutations**
25 with disease and death. Modern, scientifically **sophisticated** autopsies require **comprehensive** chemical analysis.
      In addition to their scientific applications, modern autopsies have important legal significance. An autopsy can often determine whether death was the result of foul play or natural causes. The
30 pathologist in such cases must be thorough and objective, listing all **lethal** and nonlethal facts uncovered during the examination of the body. Determining the cause of death requires a broad-based examination of the body, the scene of the death, and all related circumstances.

Words
abhorrent
comprehensive
desecration
differentiate
dissection
lethal
mutation
repugnant
sophisticated
symptom

Unlocking Meaning

Each word in this lesson's word list appears in dark print in the selection you just read. Think about how the vocabulary is used in the selection, then write the letter for the best answer to each question.

1. The best definition for *desecration* (line 3) is _____.
   (A) deep admiration (B) ridicule
   (C) the harming of something (D) removal from public view
       held sacred

1. _____

2. If something is *abhorrent* (line 4), it _____.
   (A) causes disgust and hate (B) is a source of comfort
   (C) is highly admired (D) proves one's superiority

2. _____

3. Another word for *repugnant* (line 12) is _____.
   (A) simple (B) clever
   (C) disgusting (D) alarming

3. _____

4. The word *dissection* (line 14) means _____.
   (A) separating by size (B) violent argument
   (C) exploration (D) cutting apart

4. _____

5. If you are able to *differentiate* (line 19) between two things, you
   can _____.
   (A) put them in order (B) tell the difference
   (C) place one on top of the (D) ignore one and study the
       other other

5. _____

6. A *symptom* (line 21) is a _____.
   (A) part of the body (B) sign
   (C) scientific examination (D) careful experiment

6. _____

7. Another word for *mutations* (line 24) is _____.
   (A) changes (B) colors
   (C) sounds (D) thickness

7. _____

8. A *sophisticated* autopsy (line 25) is one that is _____.
   (A) rarely performed (B) required by law
   (C) scientifically complicated (D) performed immediately
       or complex after death

8. _____

9. Another word for *comprehensive* (line 26) is _____.
   (A) thorough (B) careless
   (C) simple (D) brief

9. _____

10. *Lethal* (line 31) means _____.
    (A) legal (B) able to cause death
    (C) experimental (D) microscopic

10. _____

Applying Meaning

Follow the directions below to write a sentence using a vocabulary word.

1. Use *abhorrent* to describe something you observed, read about, or saw on television.

   _____

   _____

   _____

2. Describe a report given by a classmate. Use the word *comprehensive*.

   _____

   _____

   _____

3. Write a sentence about the uniforms players wear in a basketball game. Use the word *differentiate*.

   _____

   _____

   _____

4. Use *sophisticated* in a sentence about space exploration.

   _____

   _____

   _____

Each question below contains a vocabulary word from this lesson. Answer each question "yes" or "no" in the space provided.

5. Is each section of the country divided into smaller *dissections*?   5. _____

6. Would a doctor order a *lethal* medication for a patient with a minor illness.   6. _____

7. Is cancer a type of *mutation* in human cells?   7. _____

8. Does a game of chess or tennis require great *desecration* on the part of the players?   8. _____

9. Is sneezing one *symptom* of a cold?   9. _____

10. Does rotting garbage give off a *repugnant* odor?   10. _____

For each question you answered "no," write a sentence explaining your reason.

_____

_____

_____

_____

_____

_____

_____

_____

Mastering Meaning

Experiments involving new drugs and surgical procedures are often performed first on animals. Such experiments undoubtedly cause great pain and suffering for the animals, but often lead to the development of medicines and surgical techniques that save human lives. Write a short essay defending or criticizing the practice of using animals for experiments. Use some of the words you have studied in this lesson.

Lesson

17

Part A

Name _____

People's moods change, while their personalities are more constant. There are great varieties of moods and personalities, and the language that can be used to describe them is rich and colorful. In this lesson, you will learn ten words that describe different kinds of moods and personalities.

Unlocking Meaning

Read the sentences or short passages below. Write the letter for the correct definition of the italicized vocabulary word.

1. I can't believe that someone who was once such a show-off is now so *self-effacing*.
   - (A) willing to take credit for everything
   - (B) able to fix mechanical objects
   - (C) modest; content to stay in the background
   - (D) furious; filled with angry thoughts

2. Luckily, Theresa is not a person who is *vindictive*. She is usually willing to forgive and forget small injuries.
   - (A) filled with a need to learn
   - (B) forgetful
   - (C) hard to understand
   - (D) looking for revenge

3. People think of writers as lonely hermits, but Robert Benchley was a *sociable* sort, who enjoyed both people and parties.
   - (A) friendly
   - (B) foolish
   - (C) sloppy
   - (D) truthful

4. People who love animals become *indignant* when they see someone mistreat a helpless pet.
   - (A) homeless
   - (B) filled with joy
   - (C) angry because of something unfair or mean
   - (D) less able to remember things correctly

5. President Calvin Coolidge was said to be so *stolid* that when he died, writer Dorothy Parker asked, "How can they tell?"
   - (A) filled with cheer and good humor
   - (B) hard to excite; lacking in emotion
   - (C) unwilling to serve his country
   - (D) fearful of losing his money

Words

egotistical

indignant

reluctant

self-effacing

skeptical

snobbish

sociable

stolid

sullen

vindictive

1. _____

2. _____

3. _____

4. _____

5. _____

6. Let someone else give Carlos credit. He will seem *egotistical* if he says the project was his idea.
   - (A) concerned with numbers
   - (B) aware of danger
   - (C) reckless or lacking in common sense
   - (D) too self-centered

6. _____

7. One child became *sullen* and uncooperative when the others decided to play a different game.
   - (A) sulky and silent; quiet because of a bad mood
   - (B) eager to please someone else
   - (C) excited about the future; filled with joy
   - (D) sorry about past behavior

7. _____

8. Most scientists are *skeptical* of new theories until the ideas are proven by several people.
   - (A) full of smiles
   - (B) innocent of wrongdoing
   - (C) not able to see clearly
   - (D) filled with doubts

8. _____

9. The horse was so *reluctant* to cross the bridge that Yani had to get off, cover the animal's eyes, and lead it across.
   - (A) glad
   - (B) unwilling
   - (C) too stupid
   - (D) proud

9. _____

10. Neither candidate was *snobbish*. In spite of their money and power, they were both as polite to their drivers and household workers as they were to the mayor.
    - (A) able to forget a wrong that had been done to them
    - (B) one who looks down on people with less money or rank
    - (C) quick to begin but slow to finish
    - (D) strange in their clothing or actions

10. _____

Applying Meaning

Follow the directions below to write a sentence using a vocabulary word.

1. Tell how you would feed a cat that did not like the food you served. Use any form of the word *reluctant*.

_____

_____

_____

2. Use any form of the word *sociable* to describe someone who is invited to many parties.

_____

_____

_____

3. Use any form of the word *snobbish* to describe a new student who is shy but looks unfriendly.

_____

_____

_____

4. Use any form of the word *egotistical* to describe how an unpopular person sounds to others.

_____

_____

_____

5. Describe a person you would not want to sit next to on a bus ride. Use any form of the word *sullen*.

_____

_____

_____

Read each sentence or short passage below. Answer each question "yes" or "no" in the space provided.

6. Is a *self-effacing* person likely to seek constant applause?   6. _____

7. Is an *indignant* person likely to be smiling?   7. _____

8. Would a *vindictive* person try to get even with someone who had played a mean trick?

8. _____

9. Is a *stolid* person very likely to be the one who has partygoers laughing constantly?

9. _____

10. Would a *skeptical* person readily believe a story about alien invaders?

10. _____

For each question you answered "no," write a sentence explaining your reason.

_____

_____

_____

_____

_____

_____

_____

_____

_____

_____

_____

_____

Our Living Language

During the sixteenth century, a popular new form of theater called the *commedia dell'arte* was developed in Italy. Traveling groups of actors went from town to town putting on funny performances. Although there were many different stories, all had the same group of characters. These often included a soldier and a delicate girl. One character was named Zanni, which is the short form of Giovanni. Zanni told jokes, engaged in low humor, and generally acted silly. From his name came the word *zany*, meaning "a clown" or "someone who acts foolish to make others laugh." The word also describes actions that cause laughter.

Write a List: Identify or create a character who is zany. List some of the things that person might do.

The Prefixes *sub-* and *super-*

Name _____

The Latin word *sub,* meaning "under" or "below," gives us the English prefix *sub-*. The *subconscious* is below the level of consciousness. The Latin word *super,* meaning "above" or "over," gives us the prefix *super-*. The *supernatural* world is above or outside of the natural world.

Prefix	Meaning	English Word
sub-	under, below	subconscious
super-	above, over	supernatural

Unlocking Meaning

A vocabulary word appears in italics in each passage below. The meaning of the root is given in parentheses. Write a definition for the vocabulary word. Compare your definition with the dictionary definition at the back of the book.

1. Even though I had tickets to the game, I had a *subconscious* wish to stay home. (Root word: *scire,* "to know")

   _____

   _____

   _____

2. It took hours for rescuers to *subdue* the wild moose that had strayed onto the highway. (Root word: *ducere,* "to lead")

   _____

   _____

   _____

3. Once the Union had forced the South into *submission,* a healing of the country's wounds began. (Root word: *mittere,* "to cause to go")

   _____

   _____

   _____

4. His assistant has a *subordinate* role. He offers advice, but the coach makes all decisions. (Root word: *ordinare,* "to set in order")

   _____

   _____

   _____

Words

- **subconscious**
- **subdue**
- **submission**
- **subordinate**
- **subservient**
- **subversion**
- **superficial**
- **superimpose**
- **superlative**
- **supernatural**

5. Alicia's *subservient* behavior toward the new boss is disgusting. Did you see how she ran to get his coffee? (Root word: *servire*, "to serve")

_____

_____

_____

6. The judge ruled that the police department's search was a *subversion* of the defendant's rights. (Root word: *vertere*, "to turn")

_____

_____

_____

7. The cut on her lip was quite *superficial*. It healed completely in two days. (Root word: *facies*, "face")

_____

_____

_____

8. The detective used a computer to *superimpose* possible disguises on a picture of the suspect. (Root word: *imponere*, "to place upon")

_____

_____

_____

9. A painter, inventor, and sculptor, Da Vinci is a *superlative* example of the Renaissance man. (Root word: *latus*, carried)

_____

_____

_____

10. Some ancient kings were also worshiped as *supernatural* beings. (Root word: *natura*, "nature")

_____

_____

_____

Applying Meaning

Write a vocabulary word to complete each statement.

1. Undivided is to *subdivided* as *unconscious* is to _____.

2. Revert is to *reversion* as *subvert* is to _____.

3. Market is to *supermarket* as *natural* is to _____.

4. Greater is to *comparative* as *greatest* is to _____.

5. Sad is to *happy* as *deep* is to _____.

1. _____
2. _____
3. _____
4. _____
5. _____

Follow the directions below to write a sentence using a vocabulary word.

6. Describe a scene from a movie or television program involving the police. Use any form of the word *subdue*.

   _____

   _____

   _____

7. Use the word *superimpose* in a sentence about a trick someone plays on another person.

   _____

   _____

   _____

8. Describe the relationship between two people. Use the word *subordinate*.

   _____

   _____

   _____

9. Use *submission* in a sentence about an event in American history.

   _____

   _____

   _____

10. Complete the following statement: His *subservient* attitude was evident when he. . . .

_____

_____

_____

Test-Taking Strategies

Analogy tests require you to think carefully about how two words relate to each other and then to find the word pair that best expresses a similar relationship. Remember, you are looking for the <u>best</u> match.

Practice: Each question below consists of a pair of related words, followed by four pairs of words or phrases. Select the pair that best expresses the same relationship as the original pair.

1. WIND:SAIL   (A) rainbow:color   (B) fish:water   1. _____
                      (C) brush:paint   (D) gasoline:engine

2. DOCTOR:ILLNESS   (A) librarian:books   (B) dentist:toothache   2. _____
                          (C) teacher:school   (D) mechanic:tools

3. RECIPE:COOK   (A) uniform:soldier   (B) word:sentence   3. _____
                      (C) map:driver   (D) laboratory:chemist

Name _____

How well do you remember the words you studied in Lessons 16 through 18? Take the following test covering the words from the last three lessons.

Part 1 Choose the Correct Meaning

Each question below includes a word in capital letters, followed by four words or phrases. Choose the word or phrase that is <u>closest</u> in meaning to the word in capital letters. Write the letter for your answer on the line provided.

Sample

| S. FINISH | (A) enjoy | (B) complete | S. _____ |
| | (C) destroy | (D) enlarge | |

| 1. SULLEN | (A) glum | (B) outnumbered | 1. _____ |
| | (C) buried | (D) late | |

| 2. SUPERIMPOSE | (A) take advantage of | (B) accept | 2. _____ |
| | (C) lay over | (D) succeed | |

| 3. REPUGNANT | (A) inclined to fight | (B) overeager | 3. _____ |
| | (C) very useful | (D) strongly distasteful | |

| 4. SOCIABLE | (A) easily convinced | (B) friendly | 4. _____ |
| | (C) publicly funded | (D) anxious | |

| 5. EGOTISTICAL | (A) self-centered | (B) happy | 5. _____ |
| | (C) experienced | (D) talented | |

| 6. LETHAL | (A) sharp | (B) permissible | 6. _____ |
| | (C) level | (D) deadly | |

| 7. STOLID | (A) sentimental | (B) unemotional | 7. _____ |
| | (C) foolish | (D) huge | |

| 8. SUBORDINATE | (A) abnormal | (B) inferior | 8. _____ |
| | (C) unusual | (D) unseen | |

| 9. SUPERFICIAL | (A) shallow | (B) excessive | 9. _____ |
| | (C) likable | (D) particular | |

| 10. COMPREHENSIVE | (A) convincing | (B) intelligible | 10. _____ |
| | (C) flattering | (D) complete | |

11. SELF-EFFACING   (A) modest   (B) weak   11. _____

                         (C) careful   (D) pompous

12. SUPERLATIVE   (A) skillful   (B) excessive   12. _____

                         (C) productive   (D) the best

13. INDIGNANT   (A) concise   (B) poor   13. _____

                         (C) angry   (D) tearful

14. SKEPTICAL   (A) ignorant   (B) uncertain   14. _____

                         (C) amused   (D) noble

15. SUBMISSION   (A) obedience   (B) classification   15. _____

                         (C) separation   (D) continuity

Part 2 Matching Words and Meanings

Match the definition in Column B with the word in Column A. Write
the letter of the correct definition on the line provided.

Column A   **Column B**

16. subversion   a. overly willing to serve   16. _____

17. sophisticated   b. highly developed, advanced   17. _____

18. vindictive   c. feeling or acting superior   18. _____

19. symptom   d. a sign that something is present   19. _____

20. reluctant   e. existing in the mind but not in conscious thought   20. _____

21. dissection   f. overthrowing or destroying an authority   21. _____

22. snobbish   g. wanting revenge   22. _____

23. mutation   h. a change   23. _____

24. subservient   i. taking apart   24. _____

25. subconscious   j. unwilling   25. _____

Name _____

Paul Bunyan and the Tall Tale

There must be something about campfires that **stimulates** the storyteller in us. It was around frontier campfires that boredom and a sense of competition combined to create a **proliferation** of tall tales. Here were born such characters as Pecos Bill and John
5 Henry. Even the actions of real human beings like Davy Crockett were **enhanced** with carefully **contrived** tales of unbelievable strength and courage. Perhaps the best-known character is Paul Bunyan, the logger.

Stories of Paul Bunyan's size **abound**. One story claims that at
10 birth a huge boat served as Paul's cradle. The river gently rocked baby Paul to sleep, but when he rolled around in his bed, he created waves so large that people had to climb on their roofs to escape them. Another story **recounts** how Paul created the Grand Canyon by dragging his ax behind him as he walked across the plains.

15 The **disparity** between Paul and his surroundings occasionally caused some problems. He had to be constantly reminded not to step on houses or put his foot on a mountain to tie his shoe.

In most of the stories of Paul Bunyan, he is accompanied by his famous blue ox named Babe. Like Paul, Babe was huge. Her
20 size was a great advantage. Paul Bunyan could clear an entire forest in one morning. Before he had Babe, however, his work was **impaired** because he had no way to carry away the trees he cut down. Babe could carry all the trees in a forest on her back.

In one well-known tale, a serious water shortage occurred at a
25 logging camp in North Dakota. Paul and Babe could not stand by **impassively** while men went thirsty, so Paul tied a big tank on Babe's back and set out to get water from the Great Lakes. On their return trip, Babe's hoofs made holes in the ground, and the water from the tank spilled into them. According to the story, this is how
30 Minnesota came to have so many lakes. One **addendum** to the story concerns an accident that supposedly occurred midway through the journey. Babe tripped, and all of the water spilled out of the tank on her back. This spill was the start of the Mississippi River.

Words

- abound
- addendum
- contrived
- disparity
- enhance
- impair
- impassive
- proliferation
- recount
- stimulate

Each word in this lesson's word list appears in dark type in the selection you just read. Think about how the vocabulary word is used in the selection, then write the letter for the best answer to each question.

1. Which word could best replace *stimulates* in line 1?   1. _____
   (A) delays   (B) arouses
   (C) explains   (D) duplicates

2. A *proliferation* (line 3) is a _____.   2. _____
   (A) quiet pause   (B) way of making money
   (C) rapid increase   (D) promise

3. If you *enhance* (line 6) something, you _____.   3. _____
   (A) surround it in mystery   (B) make it greater in size or value
   (C) force it into a small space (D) explain it to someone

4. A *contrived* (line 6) tale is one that is _____.   4. _____
   (A) true in every detail (B) full of surprises
   (C) about Paul Bunyan   (D) cleverly planned

5. *Abound* (line 9) means _____.   5. _____
   (A) available in large numbers (B) go out of bounds
   (C) occurring with great   (D) disappear
       certainty

6. If you *recount* (line 13) a story, you _____.   6. _____
   (A) tell it in detail   (B) dismiss it from your memory
   (C) find it unbelievable (D) copy it into a notebook

7. Another word for *disparity* in line 15 is _____.   7. _____
   (A) mistrust   (B) love
   (C) differences   (D) similarity

8. Another word for *impaired* in line 22 is _____.   8. _____
   (A) strengthened   (B) weakened
   (C) enjoyed   (D) admired

9. If you sit around *impassively* (line 26), you _____.   9. _____
   (A) make rude remarks   (B) stay alert and attentive
   (C) make many sudden   (D) show no concern
       movements

10. An *addendum* (line 30) is _____.   10. _____
    (A) something added   (B) anything that gets attention
    (C) an explanation   (D) a mathematical term

Name _____

Applying Meaning

Decide which word in parentheses best completes the sentence. Then write the sentence, adding the missing word.

1. His reputation as a war hero _____ the candidate's chances for winning the election. (enhanced; impaired)

   _____

   _____

   _____

2. Her _____ look suggested that she was bored. (contrived; impassive)

   _____

   _____

   _____

3. The police were not sure about what happened because of the _____ in the accounts of the two witnesses. (disparity; proliferation)

   _____

   _____

   _____

4. Without rain to _____ their growth, my tomato plants will simply wither and die. (impair; stimulate)

   _____

   _____

   _____

5. The mayor moved to include a(n) _____ to the treasurer's report to explain the loss in revenue. (addendum; proliferation)

   _____

   _____

   _____

6. The assassins had a carefully _____ plot for taking over the government. (contrived; enhanced)

   _____

   _____

   _____

Each question below contains a vocabulary word from this lesson.
Answer each question "yes" or "no" in the space provided.

7. Would you expect joy and goodwill to *abound* at a holiday celebration?

7. _____

8. Is *proliferation* a type of air pollution?

8. _____

9. Could a retired sea captain *recount* many stories about life at sea?

9. _____

10. Does it take an expert mechanic to *impair* modern jet engines?

10. _____

For each question you answered "no," write a sentence explaining your reason.

_____

_____

_____

_____

_____

_____

_____

_____

_____

Mastering Meaning

Think of some geographical feature of the United States. It might be a mountain, a peninsula, or a similar feature. Make up a tall tale about Paul Bunyan or another superhuman individual to explain how that feature came into being. Use some of the words you studied in this lesson.

Name _____

Imagine trying to describe the form or shape of an airplane to someone who had never seen one. Words like *big* and *long* are not specific
enough. For this and other descriptions, we need words that define
particular forms and shapes exactly, especially in science, mathemat-
ics, art, and architecture. In this lesson you will learn ten words that
describe forms and shapes.

Unlocking Meaning

Read the sentences or short passages below. Write the letter for the
correct definition of the italicized vocabulary word.

Words
bilateral
bulbous
concave
convex
elliptical
linear
polygon
serpentine
statuesque
symmetry

1. The two countries settled their differences. Leaders on both sides
   felt they could accept the terms of their *bilateral* agreement.
   (A) one-sided   (B) two-sided
   (C) built of straight lines   (D) triangular

2. After the fighter's nose was broken several times, it began to take
   on a *bulbous* shape.
   (A) bulb-shaped   (B) rectangular
   (C) long and narrow   (D) egg-shaped

3. Rainwater collected in the *concave* surface of the ditch.
   (A) bumpy   (B) coiled
   (C) curved outward, like a dome (D) curved inward, like a bowl

4. The children began the sand castle by creating a rounded hill of
   sand. Then, with a pointed stick, they etched details into this
   convex surface.
   (A) bumpy   (B) coiled
   (C) curved outward, like a dome (D) curved inward, like a bowl

5. The *elliptical* shape of a jelly bean may cause it to slip down one's
   throat and get caught there. This is not a good candy to give
   small children.
   (A) circular   (B) oval
   (C) square   (D) two-sided

6. The *linear* dimensions of the court were 12 feet by 8 feet.
   (A) related to lines or length   (B) made up of circles
   (C) triangular   (D) long and narrow

1. _____

2. _____

3. _____

4. _____

5. _____

6. _____

7. To make street signs easier to recognize, each one appears on a different *polygon*. *Stop* appears on a six-sided sign, and *Yield* appears on a triangle.

7. _____

(A) any rough surface
(B) a flat, red surface
(C) a geometric figure with three or more straight sides
(D) a rectangle or square

8. The *serpentine* mountain road made all of us feel a little uneasy. More than once we narrowly missed one of the many sharp curves.

8. _____

(A) having many bends and curves
(B) straight and narrow
(C) wide
(D) clearly marked

9. The diver struck a *statuesque* pose on the end of the board, then gracefully floated into the air and completed a perfect dive.

9. _____

(A) short and round
(B) tall, stately, and well-proportioned
(C) lean and thin
(D) frightening

10. Greek architecture emphasized the need for *symmetry*. If one side of a building had four columns and twenty-four steps, the other side also had four columns and twenty-four steps.

10. _____

(A) unevenness
(B) long, narrow shapes
(C) perfectly balanced on two sides
(D) a simple appearance

Applying Meaning

Decide which word in parentheses best completes the sentence. Then write the sentence, adding the missing word.

1. The _____ shape of the egg made it difficult to stand it on end. (elliptical; linear)

   _____

   _____

   _____

2. The _____ honor guard stood at attention. (bulbous; statuesque)

   _____

   _____

   _____

3. Although it was ten miles long, the _____ river emptied into a lake just two miles from its source. (bilateral; serpentine)

   _____

   _____

   _____

4. Dali's painting *The Last Supper* is perfect in its _____. Its left side is a mirror image of the right. (polygon; symmetry)

   _____

   _____

   _____

5. The _____ satellite dish was designed to catch the signals from space and reflect them inward. (concave; convex)

   _____

   _____

   _____

6. Unless the negotiator could get a _____ agreement to the terms, the strike would surely continue. (bilateral; linear)

   _____

   _____

   _____

7. By comparing the building's shadow to the shadow of a ruler, we determined its _____ height. (linear; serpentine)

_____

_____

_____

Follow the directions to write a sentence using a vocabulary word.

8. Describe something using the word *bulbous*.

_____

_____

_____

9. Complete this sentence: In math class we learned how to calculate the area of several *polygons*, including. . . .

_____

_____

_____

10. Use *convex* to describe the shape of something.

_____

_____

_____

Bonus Word

Quad-

The word *triangle* contains the prefix *tri-*, which means "three."

Therefore, a triangle is a flat figure that contains three angles and three

sides. The prefix *quad-* means "four." Words with this prefix have

"four" as part of their meaning

Work with a Partner: Write a short definition for each of these words.

Use a dictionary if you need help.

quadrant   quadraphonic sound   quadrennial   quadruplicate

The Prefix ex-

Name _____

The prefix *ex-* or *e-* comes from a Latin prefix meaning "out," "outside," or "away from." This prefix is usually combined with a root to form a word. Although the meaning of the root may not be well known, knowing the prefix and its meaning will help you unlock the meaning of an unfamiliar word.

Prefix/Meaning	Root/Meaning	Word
ex- out, outside	stinguere to quench	extinct
e- away from	rodere to gnaw	erosion

Unlocking Meaning

Write the vocabulary word that fits each clue below. Then say the word and write a short definition. Compare your definition and pronunciation with those given in the dictionary at the back of the book.

1. It is the verb form of *evolution*. It contains a root from the Latin word *volvere*, meaning "to roll."

   _____

   _____

   _____

2. It comes from the same Latin word as *excellent*. In fact you can see this word in *excellent*.

   _____

   _____

   _____

3. This word is very similar to its Latin source, *exterminare*, meaning "to drive out."

   _____

   _____

   _____

4. This word is the noun form of the adjective *extreme*. Your foot is one of four that your body has.

   _____

   _____

   _____

Words

- eradicate
- erosion
- estrange
- evolve
- exacerbate
- excel
- expatriate
- exterminate
- extinct
- extremity

5. An antonym for *befriend*, the Latin source for this word means "to treat as a stranger."

_____

_____

_____

6. This "gnawing away" word can literally describe what happens to soil or figuratively what happens to someone's confidence.

_____

_____

_____

7. It describes something that is taken "away from" us forever, like the dinosaurs.

_____

_____

_____

8. This word adds the prefix *e-* to the Latin root *radix*, meaning "root." Literally, it means to "eliminate the roots."

_____

_____

_____

9. The Latin word for one's native land is *patria*. One who prefers living in a foreign country is called this.

_____

_____

_____

10. This word combines the prefix *ex-* with the Latin root *acerbare* meaning "to make harsh." Rain does this to a flood.

_____

_____

_____

Applying Meaning

Read each sentence below. Write "correct" on the answer line if the vocabulary word has been used correctly or "incorrect" if it has been used incorrectly.

1. The crowd was startled by the loud *erosion* when the supersonic jets flew overhead.

1. _____

2. Miami is located at the southernmost *extremity* of Florida.

2. _____

3. For a time, Hemingway joined a group of *expatriate* writers in Paris.

3. _____

4. Upon entering the garage, we detected the *extinct* odor of gasoline.

4. _____

5. The Salk and Sabin vaccines have nearly *eradicated* polio in the United States.

5. _____

6. The moon *evolves* around the earth.

6. _____

For each word used incorrectly, write a sentence using the word properly.

_____

_____

_____

_____

_____

_____

_____

_____

_____

_____

Follow the directions below to write a sentence using a vocabulary word.

7. Describe a relationship between two people. Use any form of the word *estrange*.

_____

_____

8. Describe the effects of a political speech on a controversial topic. Use any form of the word *exacerbate*.

_____

_____

_____

9. Use *exterminate* in a sentence about a pest.

_____

_____

_____

10. Describe an outstanding athlete. Use any form of the word *excel*.

_____

_____

_____

Using the Dictionary

A dictionary may give several meanings for a word. Sometimes a sample sentence or phrase using the word may also be provided in order to make the meaning clear. Study the sample dictionary entry below.

ex e cute (**ek'** si kyoot') *v.* **ex e cut ed, ex e cut ing, ex e cutes.**

1. To carry out: *For his final dive, Brad will attempt to execute a triple somersault.* 2. To put to death for a crime: *The state will execute the convicted murderer.*

Look up the following words in a classroom dictionary. Use each word in two sentences. The word should have a different meaning in each sentence.

deed   prominent   douse

Name _____

How well do you remember the words you studied in Lessons 19 through 21? Take the following test covering the words from the last three lessons.

Part 1 Antonyms

Each question below includes a word in capital letters, followed by four words or phrases. Choose the word or phrase that is most nearly <u>opposite</u> in meaning to the word in capital letters. Consider all choices before deciding on your answer. Write the letter for your answer on the line provided.

Sample

S. SLOW	(A) lazy	(B) simple	S. _____C_____
	(C) fast	(D) common	

1. PROLIFERATION	(A) array	(B) collection	1. _____
	(C) expanse	(D) reduction	
2. EXTREMITY	(A) surface	(B) core	2. _____
	(C) part	(D) link	
3. SERPENTINE	(A) oval	(B) straight	3. _____
	(C) shapeless	(D) snake-like	
4. IMPASSIVE	(A) passionate	(B) serious	4. _____
	(C) rude	(D) active	
5. EXACERBATE	(A) complicate	(B) consider	5. _____
	(C) discuss	(D) soothe	
6. EXCEL	(A) difficult	(B) flat	6. _____
	(C) deep	(D) lag	
7. SYMMETRY	(A) unevenness	(B) beauty	7. _____
	(C) color	(D) volume	
8. ABOUND	(A) decrease	(B) renew	8. _____
	(C) reverberate	(D) flow	
9. EXTERMINATE	(A) resolve	(B) kill	9. _____
	(C) count	(D) increase	
10. DISPARITY	(A) happiness	(B) change	10. _____
	(C) improvement	(D) similarity	

11. ESTRANGE (A) invite (B) befriend 11. _____
(C) correspond with (D) receive from

12. IMPAIR (A) couple (B) complete 12. _____
(C) improve (D) solve

13. ERADICATE (A) liberate (B) create 13. _____
(C) dismiss (D) clean

14. STIMULATE (A) copy (B) return 14. _____
(C) discourage (D) move

15. ENHANCE (A) reduce (B) increase 15. _____
(C) withdraw (D) unite

Part 2 Matching Words and Meanings

Match the definition in Column B with the word in Column A. Write the letter of the correct definition on the line provided.

Column A	Column B	
16. extinct	a. on a line	16. _____
17. bilateral	b. carefully created	17. _____
18. elliptical	c. oval-shaped	18. _____
19. addendum	d. wearing away	19. _____
20. contrived	e. dignified, well-proportioned	20. _____
21. evolve	f. addition	21. _____
22. statuesque	g. no longer existing	22. _____
23. polygon	h. figure having three or more sides	23. _____
24. erosion	i. develop over time	24. _____
25. linear	j. involving two sides	25. _____

Name _____

The Siege of Vicksburg

The Union strategy in the midst of the Civil War was simple: gain control of the Mississippi River, and the Confederacy will be broken **asunder**. Severed from its important resources lying west of this great river, Lee's eastern armies would gradually collapse. There
5   was, however, one **formidable** obstacle to this plan—Vicksburg. Called the Gibraltar[1] of the Confederacy, Vicksburg, Mississippi, offered the perfect **bastion** for the defenders. Entrenched on high bluffs overlooking a hairpin turn in the river, the forces at Vicksburg, commanded by the Union-born General John C. Pemberton, could
10   sink any ship attempting to pass and **rebuff** any assault. The task of **neutralizing** this fortress fell to Ulysses S. Grant.

Grant tried a variety of **tactics** to unseat the rebel force. The simple **expedient** of crossing upriver and approaching Vicksburg from the east was defeated by an impassable swamp. Several attempts to
15   sail down the river failed. At one point Grant even tried to dig a new channel in the river to bypass Vicksburg. Eventually he decided to march his armies south on the west bank of the river then to ferry them across below Vicksburg. Once across, he sent General W. T. Sherman east to block any efforts to reinforce the now-endangered
20   **citadel**. Grant's huge siege guns began to bombard the isolated city with artillery.

Little by little the army and the civilian population of Vicksburg exhausted their supplies of food and ammunition. Instead of chicken or pork, small amounts of mule meat were **rationed** to the hungry
25   defenders.

Finding his position **untenable**, Pemberton decided to surrender Vicksburg on July 4, 1863. By laying down his arms on this Union holiday, he hoped to gain more generous terms from Grant. It was eighty-five years before Vicksburg celebrated the Fourth of July.

Words
asunder
bastion
citadel
expedient
formidable
neutralize
ration
rebuff
tactic
untenable

---

[1] A three-mile peninsula dominated by a 1,396-foot cliff on the southern tip of Spain. It guards the entrance to the Mediterranean Sea.

Each word in this lesson's word list appears in dark type in the selection you just read. Think about how the vocabulary word is used in the selection, then write the letter for the best answer to each question.

1. Another word for **asunder** in line 3 is _____.
   (A) together   (B) apart
   (C) accidentally   (D) slightly

   1. _____

2. A **formidable** (line 5) obstacle is one that is _____.
   (A) oddly shaped   (B) simple
   (C) quickly thrown together (D) difficult to defeat

   2. _____

3. A **bastion** (line 7) is a _____.
   (A) heavily defended position (B) source of food
   (C) disagreeable person   (D) deep valley

   3. _____

4. If you **rebuff** (line 10) something, you _____.
   (A) polish it   (B) drive it away
   (C) embrace it   (D) examine it carefully

   4. _____

5. If you **neutralize** (line 11) a fortress, you _____.
   (A) make an enemy of it   (B) bargain with it
   (C) make it powerless   (D) surrender to it

   5. _____

6. **Tactics** (line 12) can best be described as _____.
   (A) systems for sending   (B) a series of pauses to allow
       messages   armies to regroup
   (C) offers of assistance (D) plans for meeting a goal

   6. _____

7. An **expedient** (line 13) is a(n) _____.
   (A) way of achieving a desired (B) areas that have been expanded
       result
   (C) type of weapon used in   (D) scouting party
       naval combat

   7. _____

8. A **citadel** (line 20) is a _____.
   (A) source of water for a city (B) a small raiding party
   (C) a stronghold at or near a city (D) type of celebration

   8. _____

9. If food is **rationed**, (line 24) it is _____.
   (A) allowed to become rotten (B) heavily seasoned
   (C) given out in limited amounts (D) hidden to avoid capture by
                                         an enemy

   9. _____

10. Another word for **untenable** (line 26) is _____.
    (A) strengthened   (B) indefensible
    (C) invisible   (D) elevated

    10. _____

Applying Meaning

Read each sentence below. Write "correct" on the answer line if the vocabulary word has been used correctly or "incorrect" if it has been used incorrectly.

1. The lightning split *asunder* the trunk of the mighty oak tree.

1. _____

2. Hurricane Bob caused *untenable* damage to the homes of anyone living near the shore.

2. _____

3. The hero was awarded the nation's highest *citadel* in an impressive ceremony.

3. _____

4. Elderly residents were urged to drink lots of water to *neutralize* the effects of the heat wave.

4. _____

5. In history class we studied Richard Byrd's *expedient* to the polar regions of the Antarctic.

5. _____

6. The courts are the last *bastion* of hope for the powerless in a free and just society.

6. _____

For each word used incorrectly, write a sentence using the word properly.

_____

_____

_____

_____

_____

_____

_____

_____

_____

_____

_____

_____

_____

_____

_____

_____

_____

Follow the directions below to write a sentence using a vocabulary word.

7. Describe a crisis or emergency. Use any form of the word *ration*.

_____

_____

_____

8. Use *formidable* in a sentence about a problem you or someone
   you know encountered.

_____

_____

_____

9. Write a sentence about how you approached a problem. Use any
   form of the word *tactic*.

_____

_____

_____

10. Describe a real or imaginary battle. Use any form of the word *rebuff*.

_____

_____

_____

Mastering Meaning

Imagine that you are General Grant on July 5, 1863. Vicksburg has
surrendered, and you now hold all of the Mississippi River. Write a
report to your commander-in-chief, Abraham Lincoln, describing your
success. Include some information on how you managed to achieve a
victory and what it means for the war effort. Use some of the words
you studied in this lesson.

Name _____

The English language sometimes uses the name of a person or place to describe something associated with that person or place. For example, an *atlas* is a book of maps. Its name comes from the Greek god Atlas. Because Atlas attempted to overthrow Zeus, the king of the gods, he was forced to spend the rest of his life holding the world on his shoulders. *Atlas* has come to mean "a book of the world's maps." In this lesson, you will learn ten words that have come from the names of people or places.

Unlocking Meaning

Read the sentences or short passages below. Write the letter for the correct definition of the italicized vocabulary word.

Words
babel
jovial
Lilliputian
limerick
narcissism
pandemonium
quisling
sadistic
tantalize
utopian

1. All of the children called out the answer at once. The kindergarten teacher could not make sense of such *babel*.
   (A) murmur
   (B) ringing, somewhat like a bell
   (C) confusing blend of many voices or sounds
   (D) crying or wailing

   1. _____

2. His *jovial* laugh, ready smile, and desire to make learning fun made Mr. Ames my favorite teacher.
   (A) stern
   (B) highly educated; brilliant
   (C) silly or irresponsible
   (D) full of playful good humor

   2. _____

3. In my dream, I landed in a village full of miniature houses owned by *Lilliputian* people.
   (A) cold
   (B) needy
   (C) tiny
   (D) suspicious

   3. _____

4. Hannah's *limerick* began simply enough with the lines "I once saw a monkey named Phil, who slept on the side of a hill." By the time she finished, we were doubled up with laughter.
   (A) sad story
   (B) funny poem
   (C) opera
   (D) polite request

   4. _____

5. My sister's *narcissism* is beginning to get on my nerves. She sits for hours in front of a mirror, admiring herself.
   (A) self-love
   (B) feelings of disappointment
   (C) envy or jealousy
   (D) cruelty or meanness

   5. _____

6. When the rock star asked people to join him on stage, *pandemonium* 6. _____
   broke out as scores of people ran down the aisles.
   (A) agreement   (B) disagreement
   (C) laughter   (D) wild disorder

7. Few citizens accepted the new governor general even though he
   was one of them. Instead they saw him as a *quisling* who followed
   the orders of the invaders.   7. _____
   (A) travel agent   (B) traitor
   (C) colleague   (D) hero

8. Some thought she was a superb dog trainer, but to me the use of
   a whip and a choke collar seemed *sadistic*.   8. _____
   (A) successful   (B) thought-provoking
   (C) pleasant   (D) extremely cruel

9. The smell of baking bread *tantalized* people as they walked past
   the bakery. Only the strongest could resist going inside and buying   9. _____
   a loaf.
   (A) surprised or delighted (B) teased
   (C) misled   (D) disgusted

10. The settlers hoped to create a *utopian* community in which
    everyone shared the work and the profits equally and fairly.
    (A) impractical   (B) fictional   10. _____
    (C) perfect   (D) temporary

Applying Meaning

Each question below contains at least one vocabulary word from this lesson. Answer each question "yes" or "no" in the space provided.

1. Would it be wise to *tantalize* a hungry bear by holding up a nice, fresh salmon?

2. Is Benedict Arnold an early example of a *quisling*?

3. Would you want a *Lilliputian* athlete in the starting lineup of your football team?

4. Are movie stars more likely to suffer from *narcissism* than other people are?

5. In a *utopian* world, would all people get along with one another?

6. Is *pandemonium* a rare metal found only in mountains?

1. _____

2. _____

3. _____

4. _____

5. _____

6. _____

For each question you answered "no," write a sentence explaining your reason.

_____

_____

_____

_____

_____

_____

_____

_____

_____

_____

_____

_____

Decide which word in parentheses best completes the sentence. Then write the sentence, adding the missing word.

7. To me the lyrics of the rock song were like poetry. To my father they were _____. (babel; sadistic)

_____

_____

_____

8. In some myths, Zeus is described as a harsh ruler, but other myths portray him as _____ and friendly. (jovial; utopian)

_____

_____

_____

9. Have you heard the _____ that begins, "There was a young man from Mobile"? (quisling; limerick)

_____

_____

_____

10. The activists pledged to put an end to the _____ metal traps used to catch wolves. (jovial; sadistic)

_____

_____

_____

Bonus Word

Donnybrook

Once a year a fair was held in Donnybrook, Ireland, a suburb of Dublin. This fair became well-known for the fights and large-scale brawls that broke out there. The town's name came to be associated with such brawls. Today *donnybrook* means "an uproar or large, free-for-all fight."

Cooperative Learning: Work with a partner to find the definitions and the word origins of these words: *saxophone, sideburns, cardigan, sandwich.*

Name _____

The Latin word *ab*, meaning "off" or "away" is the source of the English prefix *ab-*. In modern English this prefix may have a slightly broader, but similar, meaning. For example, in *abnormal* the *ab-* prefix means "not" normal. This differs slightly from "away from" the normal, which the prefix would suggest. Always use context clues as well as your knowledge of prefixes and roots to arrive at the meaning of an unfamiliar word.

Prefix	Root/Word	Word
ab-	normal	abnormal
ab-	tenere	abstain

Unlocking Meaning

A vocabulary word appears in italics in each passage below. The meaning of the root is given in parentheses. Look at the prefix and think about how the word is used in the passage. Then write a definition for the vocabulary word. Compare your definition with the dictionary definition at the back of the book.

1. In order to marry a divorcée, Edward VIII had to *abdicate* his throne and give up his royal title. (Root word: *dicare*, "to proclaim")

   _____

   _____

   _____

2. The senator resigned because he had come to *abhor* the constant need to raise money for his campaigns. (Root word: *horrere*, "to shudder")

   _____

   _____

   _____

3. The condition of the animals was an *abomination*. They lived in filth and most were sick. (Root word: *abominari*, "to disapprove of")

   _____

   _____

   _____

Words
- **abdicate**
- **abhor**
- **abomination**
- **aborigine**
- **abort**
- **abrasive**
- **abrupt**
- **absolute**
- **abstain**
- **abuse**

4. The government realized that the *aborigine* people held an important link to the past. (Root word: *origo*, "beginning")

_____

_____

_____

5. The pilot could not confirm that the runway was clear, so she had to *abort* the landing. (Root word: *orini*, "to appear")

_____

_____

_____

6. Never use an *abrasive* cleaner on an automobile. It will leave small scratches. (Root word: *radere*, "to scrape")

_____

_____

_____

7. The storm caused an *abrupt* change in the temperature. It suddenly dropped 20 degrees.(Root word: *rumpere*, "to break")

_____

_____

_____

8. The man promised the *absolute* truth. He had no reason to lie or withhold information. (Root word: *solvere*, "to loosen")

_____

_____

_____

9. Both candidates pledged to *abstain* from personal attacks and discuss the issues. (Root word: *tenere*, "to hold")

_____

_____

_____

10. The principal warned students not to *abuse* their library privileges by talking or sleeping. (Root word: *uti*, "to use")

_____

_____

_____

Applying Meaning

Read each sentence below. Write "correct" on the answer line if the vocabulary word has been used correctly or "incorrect" if it has been used incorrectly.

1. Upon hearing the verdict, the accused man became violent. It took several officers to *abstain* him.

1. _____

2. Even though England still has a king or queen, these rulers long ago *abdicated* their unlimited powers.

2. _____

3. The audience expected an entertaining speech, but instead the chairman *abhorred* his listeners with a financial report.

3. _____

4. The astronauts had *absolute* trust in the project's director. They knew there was a good reason for his request.

4. _____

5. The pottery held important clues about the *aborigines* who inhabited the area centuries ago.

5. _____

6. Use a sponge or dry cloth to *abuse* the gasoline before it gets into the drain and becomes a danger.

6. _____

For each word used incorrectly, write a sentence using the word properly.

_____

_____

_____

_____

_____

_____

_____

_____

_____

_____

Follow the directions below to write a sentence using a vocabulary word.

7. Describe a time when you changed your mind about something. Use any form of the word *abrupt*.

_____

_____

_____

8. Tell about something you saw or learned that shocked you. Use the word *abomination*.

_____

_____

_____

9. Use the word *abrasive* in a sentence describing how to do something.

_____

_____

_____

10. Tell about an action you or someone else took. Use the word *abort*.

_____

_____

_____

Test-Taking Strategies

Some schools require students to take a test of standard English grammar, usage, and mechanics. This test is often used to place students in the appropriate English course. When taking such a test, always read the entire sentence before deciding on your answer. If you think you have found the error, ask yourself how you would correct it.

Practice: Write the letter for the underlined part of the sentence with an error. If there is no error, write E.

1. If <u>you</u> get to the movies before Jenny and <u>I</u>, please save
   A   B
Jenny and <u>me</u> a seat <u>near the front</u>. <u>No Error</u>
        C   D   E

1. _____

2. Jonathan<u>,</u> one of our best athletes, told the coach he
      A   B
<u>would score</u> the touchdown all by <u>hisself</u> if necessary.
    C   D
<u>No Error</u>
   E

2. _____

3. The committee <u>to review</u> the new <u>books will</u> be <u>made up</u> of
                A   B   C
Jim, Olivia, and <u>myself</u>. <u>No Error</u>
             D   E

3. _____

Name _____

How well do you remember the words you studied in Lessons 22 through 24? Take the following test covering the words from the last three lessons.

Part 1 Choose the Correct Meaning

Each question below includes a word in capital letters, followed by four words or phrases. Choose the word or phrase that is <u>closest</u> in meaning to the word in capital letters. Write the letter for your answer on the line provided.

Sample

S. FINISH	(A) enjoy (C) destroy	(B) complete (D) enlarge	S. ___**B**___

1. ABHOR	(A) hate (C) support	(B) renounce (D) question	1. _____
2. PANDEMONIUM	(A) all-knowing (C) lengthy	(B) restrained (D) confusion	2. _____
3. RATION	(A) reason (C) earn	(B) measure out (D) supply	3. _____
4. ABDICATE	(A) appoint (C) retrieve	(B) give up (D) sell	4. _____
5. UNTENABLE	(A) forgivable (C) indefensible	(B) uncertain (D) forgotten	5. _____
6. ASUNDER	(A) sincerely (C) partially	(B) quickly (D) apart	6. _____
7. UTOPIAN	(A) ideal (C) new	(B) democratic (D) simple	7. _____
8. ABSOLUTE	(A) undeniable (C) complete	(B) unbelievable (D) incomprehensible	8. _____
9. BASTION	(A) fortification (C) training ground	(B) commissary (D) supply house	9. _____
10. ABRUPT	(A) sudden (C) desired	(B) useful (D) expected	10. _____

11. ABRASIVE   (A) new   (B) weak   11. _____
                    (C) cheap   (D) harsh

12. QUISLING   (A) cheapskate   (B) traitor   12. _____
                    (C) coward   (D) clever

13. LILLIPUTIAN   (A) beautiful   (B) tricky   13. _____
                    (C) tiny   (D) numerous

14. REBUFF   (A) reject   (B) polish   14. _____
                    (C) alter   (D) defeat

15. JOVIAL   (A) drunken   (B) obese   15. _____
                    (C) silly   (D) jolly

Part 2 Matching Words and Meanings

Match the definition in Column B with the word in Column A. Write the letter of the correct definition on the line provided.

Column A	Column B	
16. neutralize	a. tease	16. _____
17. abstain	b. refrain from	17. _____
18. narcissism	c. horror	18. _____
19. sadistic	d. fortress	19. _____
20. abort	e. self-love	20. _____
21. tantalize	f. offset	21. _____
22. tactic	g. hard to defeat	22. _____
23. citadel	h. to stop	23. _____
24. abomination	i. plan	24. _____
25. formidable	j. cruel	25. _____

Name _____

Tropical Rain Forests

Rain forests were once thought to be little more than bothersome **encumbrances** to exploration and civilized development. This is no longer the case. Today people throughout the world are beginning to realize that a rich variety of plants and animals are shel-
5 tered in the rain forests. Like a desert, a tropical rain forest is a **biome** with its own unique climate, plants, and animals.

Trees that grow up to 150 feet in height form a canopy that holds most of the food sources for the animals that live in them. Tropical mammals who live at these heights have learned a variety
10 of ways to move about. Gibbons and spider monkeys swing from branch to branch while other animals make **stupendous** leaps from one tree to another. For extra **stability**, tropical porcupines and monkeys wrap their tails around branches.

Sandwiched between the forest floor and the treetops is a layer
15 of natural growth called the *understory*. The dim light at this level has been filtered through the forest's canopy. Here thin-trunked trees sprout leaves that look like partially closed umbrellas which have been bent to catch the scarce sunlight. Leaf-eating animals **forage** on these lush, leafy trees. The trees also attract insect-eating
20 birds that travel the tree trunks and **ferret** out the insects that are dining on the rotting wood.

The cool, **dank** forest floor is blanketed with moss and wet leaves. Only 1 percent of the sunlight shining on the canopy reaches the ground. The **luxuriant** vegetation includes rare and
25 strange flowers and other plants, many of which have medicinal value. Two-thirds of the medicines used today were first made from rain forest plants.

Many animals lay hidden among the layers of leaves and moss. A close look reveals the natural **camouflage** that helps conceal
30 them. A leopard's **dappled** coat keeps it well hidden in the shad-ows, while the leafy-looking shell of a matamata turtle blends in with dead leaves floating down a stream.

Words
biome
camouflage
dank
dappled
encumbrance
ferret
forage
luxuriant
stability
stupendous

Unlocking Meaning

Each word in this lesson's word list appears in dark type in the selection you just read. Think about how the vocabulary word is used in the selection, then write the letter for the best answer to each question.

1. An *encumbrance* (line 2) can best be described as _____.
   (A) a type of jungle plant
   (B) something that stands in the way
   (C) a plan for developing a resource
   (D) a form of assistance

   1. _____

2. A *biome* (line 5) is a _____.
   (A) type of medicine
   (B) native tribe
   (C) explanation
   (D) natural community

   2. _____

3. A *stupendous* (line 11) performance is one that is _____.
   (A) tremendous
   (B) terrible
   (C) terrifying
   (D) rare

   3. _____

4. Another word for *stability* (line 12) would be _____.
   (A) shelter
   (B) money
   (C) firmness
   (D) amusement

   4. _____

5. When animals *forage* (line 19) they _____.
   (A) destroy forest lands
   (B) hide
   (C) attack viciously
   (D) search for food

   5. _____

6. To *ferret* (line 20) is _____.
   (A) to uncover
   (B) to frighten
   (C) to cover
   (D) to help

   6. _____

7. Another word for *dank* in line 22 is _____.
   (A) dry
   (B) colorful
   (C) damp
   (D) dangerous

   7. _____

8. *Luxuriant* (line 24) vegetation is _____.
   (A) expensive
   (B) thick and abundant
   (C) thin and yellowed
   (D) in need of water

   8. _____

9. *Camouflage* (line 29) helps animals _____.
   (A) remain hidden from other animals
   (B) find their dens
   (C) sense changes in the weather
   (D) digest their food

   9. _____

10. A *dappled* (line 30) egg is _____.
    (A) cracked
    (B) speckled
    (C) cooked
    (D) oddly shaped

    10. _____

Applying Meaning

Read each sentence below. Write "correct" on the answer line if the vocabulary word has been used correctly or "incorrect" if it has been used incorrectly.

1. The *dappled* coat of a Dalmatian makes it easy to pick out in a crowd of other dogs.

   1. _____

2. It took a great deal of *encumbrance* from his wife before FDR decided to run for president.

   2. _____

3. Cactus, rattlesnakes, and intense heat are all part of the desert *biome*.

   3. _____

4. Mushrooms grow best in a *dank* environment. That is why I raise mine in our basement.

   4. _____

5. Without a compass or map, the child soon became lost in the dark *forage*.

   5. _____

6. The gifted acrobats performed *stupendous* feats of agility.

   6. _____

For each word used incorrectly, write a sentence using the word properly.

_____

_____

_____

_____

_____

_____

_____

_____

_____

_____

_____

_____

Follow the directions below to write a sentence using a vocabulary word.

7. Use any form of the word *stability* in a sentence about a table.

_____

_____

_____

8. Use *luxuriant* in a sentence to describe something that grows.

_____

_____

_____

9. Use any form of the word *camouflage* in a sentence about something you cannot find.

_____

_____

_____

10. Use any form of the word *ferret* in a sentence about a problem you solved.

_____

_____

_____

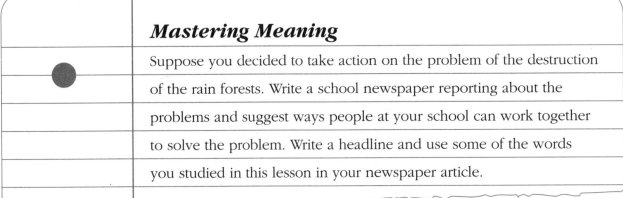

Mastering Meaning

Suppose you decided to take action on the problem of the destruction of the rain forests. Write a school newspaper reporting about the problems and suggest ways people at your school can work together to solve the problem. Write a headline and use some of the words you studied in this lesson in your newspaper article.

Name _____

Like the fields of law and government, the field of banking has its own vocabulary. When opening an account, applying for a loan, or reading your monthly statement, you will need to understand this vocabulary. In this lesson you will learn ten useful banking terms.

Unlocking Meaning

Read the sentences or short passages below. Write the letter for the correct definition of the italicized vocabulary word.

Words

appraise

assets

compound interest

cosigner

creditor

debit

default

foreclose

liability

lien

1. Before agreeing to loan Ms. Amico money to buy a new house, the bank wanted to *appraise* it. This way, the bank would be assured that the house was worth the money they were lending for it.
   (A) visit   (B) judge the value of
   (C) measure   (D) repair

2. Before drawing up his will, Mr. Donato reviewed his *assets*. They included his house, a savings account, and a new car.
   (A) things of value   (B) expenses
   (C) items bought with (D) desirable gifts
       borrowed money

1. _____

3. To make the most of a savings account, get one that pays *compound interest*. Such an account pays more than one with just simple interest.
   (A) fee based on the cost of   (B) charge for using a bank's
       living   services
   (C) money paid on money   (D) penalty for a late payment
       previously earned in a
       savings account

2. _____

4. When Hilda applied for a car loan, the bank was concerned that she might not be able to make her monthly payments. Therefore, they requested that she have a *cosigner* to share the responsibility for the loan.
   (A) legal advisor   (B) close friend or relative
   (C) bank official who processes (D) someone whose signature
       loan applications   guarantees that a loan will
                                       be paid

3. _____

4. _____

5. As your *creditor,* I am extremely pleased that you have never been late with your monthly payments.

    (A) one to whom money is owed   (B) someone with a poor credit history

    (C) a person who owes someone money   (D) a bank teller

5. _____

6. Martin withdrew $50 from his savings account, so his next bank statement showed a *debit* of $50.

    (A) error in a bank statement   (B) deduction from an account

    (C) money deposited into one's bank account   (D) deposit into a savings account

6. _____

7. A sudden drop in sales at his shop caused Mr. Jenkins to *default* on his bank loan.

    (A) fail to pay money owed   (B) offer to pay money owed

    (C) increase in an amount   (D) request that the terms of a loan be changed

7. _____

8. The bank officer warned the owners of the neglected property that unless the overdue payments were received, she would be forced to *foreclose.*

    (A) cancel a loan   (B) increase the amount owed

    (C) take a property to satisfy a loan   (D) sell the loan to another bank

8. _____

9. Ms. Talston was able to pay off the loans on her car and her refrigerator. Now she had just one remaining *liability*—the money she still owed on her home loan.

    (A) an obligation to pay a debt   (B) the total value of everything one owns

    (C) a bill that another person has agreed to pay   (D) a mistake or problem

9. _____

10. Mr. Rowe owed the heating-oil company several hundred dollars. Because the company feared that he might never pay the debt, its treasurer decided to put a *lien* on Mr. Rowe's house.

    (A) service charge   (B) meter that measures the amount of oil used monthly

    (C) type of lock   (D) right to hold something to ensure payment of a loan debt

10. _____

Applying Meaning

Each question below contains a vocabulary word from this lesson.
Answer each question "yes" or "no" in the space provided.

1. Could a bank *foreclose* on a loan that has been paid faithfully?   1. _____

2. Would most people like to have many *creditors?*   2. _____

3. Would a bank be more willing to lend you money if you had a
   cosigner?   3. _____

4. Is it preferable to have more *assets* than *liabilities?*   4. _____

5. Could a homeowner put a *lien* on his or her own property?   5. _____

6. Would a bank encourage a borrower to *default?*   6. _____

For each question you answered "no," write a sentence explaining
your reason.

_____

_____

_____

_____

_____

_____

_____

_____

_____

_____

_____

_____

_____ _____

Decide which word in parentheses best completes the sentence. Then
write the sentence adding the missing word.

7. The bank inspectors _____ the property at approximately $100,000.
   (defaulted; appraised)

_____

_____

_____

8. Banks require a business to have enough real estate or other _____ to guarantee repayment of a loan. (assets; liabilities)

_____

_____

_____

9. Jamie was quite pleased to learn that the bank paid _____ on savings accounts. (debit; compound interest)

_____

_____

_____

10. The charge for preprinted checks will appear as a _____ on your monthly statement.(debit; lien)

_____

_____

_____

Bonus Words

ATM

Sometimes we use just the initials in place of long words. We say the letters ATM instead of the more cumbersome "automatic teller machine." If the initials are pronounced like a word, the name is called an *acronym*. For example, the initials of the North Atlantic Treaty Alliance make the acronym NATO, pronounced **nā′tō**.

Match the Terms: Match the initials or acronym in the first column with a name in the second column. Circle the term that is an acronym.

ETA	revolutions per minute
PA	bacon, lettuce, and tomato sandwich
OPEC	estimated time of arrival
RPM	Organization of Petroleum Exporting Countries
BLT	physician's assistant

The Prefix in-

Name _____

The Latin prefix *in-,* meaning "not" is one of the most common prefixes in English. It is often combined with a word to reverse the meaning of the word. *Inconspicuous* means the opposite of *conspicuous.* If
the word to which the prefix is attached begins with the letter *r,* however, the prefix is said to be absorbed and its spelling changes to *ir-.*

Prefix	Word	New Word
in-	conspicuous	inconspicuous
in-	rational	irrational

Unlocking Meaning

A vocabulary word appears in italics in each sentence or short passage
below. Find the prefix in the vocabulary word and think about how the
word is used in the passage. Then write a definition for the vocabulary
word. Compare your definition with the definition in the dictionary at
the back of the book.

1. After seeing the evidence, the talkative defendant became
   inarticulate, making sounds but saying nothing.

   _____

   _____

   _____

2. The launch of the space shuttle was delayed for days by the
   inclement weather at the launch site.

   _____

   _____

   _____

3. The famous actress put on dark glasses and carried a camera in
   an effort to be *inconspicuous* in the crowd.

   _____

   _____

   _____

Words

inarticulate

inclement

inconspicuous

indiscreet

invulnerable

irrational

irredeemable

irrefutable

irrelevant

irretrievable

4. Most members felt Phil's *indiscreet* comments about the chairman's wife had ruined an otherwise cordial meeting.

_____

_____

_____

5. The Confederate position behind the stone wall atop a steep hill made it *invulnerable* to General Burnsides's attack.

_____

_____

_____

6. His *irrational* fear of spiders may have had its beginnings in some childhood event.

_____

_____

_____

7. The minister believes there is no such a thing as an *irredeemable* sinner. He feels that everyone is basically good.

_____

_____

_____

8. Even though certain *irrefutable* evidence pointed to the defendant's guilt, the lawyer promised an energetic defense.

_____

_____

_____

9. Emily felt the employer's questions about her family were *irrelevant*. They had nothing to do with the job.

_____

_____

_____

10. The keys were *irretrievable* because they fell over the side of the boat.

_____

_____

_____

Name _____

Applying Meaning

Each question below contains a vocabulary word from this lesson.
Answer each question "yes" or "no" in the space provided.

1. Would a political party want an *inarticulate* candidate for
   president?

2. Is an *irrational* cook one that has run out of food?

3. Are coupons *irredeemable* if they were to be used before
   December 31, 1997?

4. If you were accused of a crime, would you welcome *irrefutable*
   evidence of your guilt?

1. _____

2. _____

3. _____

4. _____

For each question you answered "no," write a sentence explaining
your reason.

_____

_____

_____

_____

_____

_____

_____

_____

Decide which word in parentheses best completes the sentence. Then
write the sentence, adding the missing word.

5. The spy learned the customs of the enemy so she would be _____
   as she moved among them. (inconspicuous; irrelevant)

_____

_____

_____

6. Hal's _____ remark about women in politics could cost him the
   election. (inclement; indiscreet)

_____

_____

_____

7. The cost of the yacht was _____. The wealthy sheik wanted the finest boat that money could buy. (invulnerable; irrelevant)

_____

_____

_____

8. The hard shell of the armadillo makes it nearly _____, even to larger and stronger animals. (invulnerable; inconspicuous)

_____

_____

_____

9. The _____ weather lasted for ten days. (inclement; indiscreet)

_____

_____

_____

10. The condition of the sunken battleship made the bodies of the lost sailors _____. (invulnerable; irretrievable)

_____

_____

_____

Our Living Language

in-, im-, il-

The prefix *in-* appears in more words than you may realize. You have seen how the spelling changes to *ir-* when the prefix is added to words or roots beginning with the letter *r*. The spelling changes to *im-* when *in-* is added to words or roots beginning with *b*, *m*, or *p* and to *il-* before words or roots beginning with *l*.

Build New Words: Add a form of the prefix *in-* to each of these words to create a new word that means the opposite of the original word.

in- + pure =	in- + legitimate =	in- + mobile =
in- + legal =	in- + mature =	in- + personal =
in- + potent =	in- + balance =	in- + prudent =

Name _____

How well do you remember the words you studied in Lessons 25 through 27? Take the following test covering the words from the last three lessons.

Part 1 Antonyms

Each question below includes a word in capital letters, followed by four words or phrases. Choose the word or phrase that is most nearly <u>opposite</u> in meaning to the word in capital letters. Write the letter for your answer on the line provided.

Sample

S. SLOW	(A) lazy	(B) simple	S. _____C_____
	(C) fast	(D) common	

1. INDISCREET	(A) careful	(B) slow	1. _____
	(C) secretive	(D) late	
2. DANK	(A) self-contained	(B) noisy	2. _____
	(C) dirty	(D) dry	
3. COMPOUND INTEREST	(A) low interest	(B) variable interest	3. _____
	(C) simple interest	(D) high interest	
4. INARTICULATE	(A) silent	(B) musical	4. _____
	(C) well-spoken	(D) creative	
5. INCLEMENT	(A) unexpected	(B) balmy	5. _____
	(C) hazy	(D) unpredictable	
6. STUPENDOUS	(A) bright	(B) ordinary	6. _____
	(C) complex	(D) colorful	
7. IRRELEVANT	(A) fitting	(B) respectful	7. _____
	(C) calm	(D) forgetful	
8. IRRETRIEVABLE	(A) shallow	(B) valuable	8. _____
	(C) new	(D) recoverable	
9. ASSETS	(A) hopes	(B) skills	9. _____
	(C) debts	(D) accounts	
10. INCONSPICUOUS	(A) easy to use	(B) left behind	10. _____
	(C) noticeable	(D) hidden from view	

11. IRRATIONAL	(A) excited	(B) complicated	11. _____	
	(C) mature	(D) logical		
12. ENCUMBRANCE	(A) hurdle	(B) assistance	12. _____	
	(C) goal	(D) tool		
13. INVULNERABLE	(A) defenseless	(B) hospitable	13. _____	
	(C) ready	(D) without merit		
14. IRREFUTABLE	(A) complete	(B) expected	14. _____	
	(C) questionable	(D) usual		
15. DEBIT	(A) deduction	(B) credit	15. _____	
	(C) balance	(D) fee		

Part 2 Matching Words and Meanings

Match the definition in Column B with the word in Column A. Write
the letter of the correct definition on the line provided.

Column A	Column B	
16. camouflage	a. lush, abundant	16. _____
17. foreclose	b. disguise	17. _____
18. lien	c. failure to pay a debt	18. _____
19. forage	d. property held to pay a loan	19. _____
20. luxuriant	e. hunt	20. _____
21. appraise	f. assess the value of	21. _____
22. biome	g. take to satisfy a debt	22. _____
23. liability	h. spotted	23. _____
24. default	i. natural community	24. _____
25. dappled	j. obligation	25. _____

Name _____

Mark Twain's First Appearance

Besides being an **eminent** author, Mark Twain was also a talented speaker, who told stories to audiences with the same **shrewd** humor he showed in his fiction. On one occasion, Twain related a personal **anecdote** about stage fright. It seems he was attending his daugh-
5   ter's first singing performance, when the audience **cajoled** him into speaking. With no prepared speech in mind, Twain gave an **impromptu** talk about the steps he took to **ensure** success during his own first appearance on stage. Here is a portion of that talk:

I had got a number of friends of mine, stalwart men, to
10   sprinkle themselves through the audience armed with big clubs. Every time I said anything they could possibly guess I intended to be funny, they were to pound those clubs on the floor. Then there was a kind lady in a box up there, also a good friend of mine, the wife of the governor. She was to
15   watch me **intently**, and whenever I glanced toward her she was going to deliver a gubernatorial laugh that would lead the whole audience into applause.

At last I began. I had the **manuscript** tucked under a United States flag in front of me where I could get at it in case
20   of need. But I managed to get started without it. I walked up and down—I was young in those days and needed the exer-cise—and talked and talked.

Right in the middle of the speech I had placed a gem. I had put in a moving, pathetic part which was to get at the
25   hearts and souls of my hearers. When I delivered it, they did just what I hoped and expected. They sat silent and **awed**. I had touched them. Then I happened to look up at the box where the governor's wife was—you know what happened.

Well, after the first **agonizing** five minutes, my stage fright
30   left me, never to return. . . . But I shall never forget my feel-ings before the agony left me, and I got up here to thank you for helping my daughter, by your kindness, to live through her first appearance. And I want to thank you for your appre-ciation of her singing, which is, by the way, hereditary.

Words

agonize

anecdote

awe

cajole

eminent

ensure

impromptu

intently

manuscript

shrewd

Each word in this lesson's word list appears in dark type in the selection you just read. Think about how the vocabulary word is used in the selection, then write the letter for the best answer to each question.

1. Which word could best replace *eminent* in line 1?
   (A) humorous   (B) old
   (C) famous   (D) unknown

            1. _____

2. Which word could best replace *shrewd* in line 2?
   (A) rapid   (B) quick-witted
   (C) shy   (D) quick-tempered

            2. _____

3. An *anecdote* (line 4) is best described as _____.
   (A) an account of an event   (B) a prepared speech
   (C) joke   (D) commercial

            3. _____

4. To *cajole* (line 5) is to _____.
   (A) urge gently   (B) demand
   (C) applaud   (D) ridicule

            4. _____

5. An *impromptu* (line 7) speech is one that is _____.
   (A) filled with slanderous   (B) meant for a presidential
       language   candidate
   (C) not prepared in advance   (D) prepared in advance

            5. _____

6. In line 7 *ensure* means _____.
   (A) boast   (B) deny
   (C) make certain   (D) make worse

            6. _____

7. When a person looks *intently* (line 15), he or she looks _____.
   (A) casually   (B) questioningly
   (C) with concern   (D) with close attention

            7. _____

8. A *manuscript* (line 18) is a _____.
   (A) handwritten document or   (B) envelope
       book
   (C) machine   (D) container of money

            8. _____

9. Another word for *awed* (line 26) is _____.
   (A) dreaded   (B) ashamed
   (C) chilled   (D) astounded

            9. _____

10. *Agonizing* (line 29) is best described as _____.
   (A) binding   (B) moving
   (C) painful   (D) noticeable

          10. _____

Applying Meaning

Follow the directions below to write a sentence using a vocabulary word.

1. Use the word *eminent* to describe someone.

   _____

   _____

   _____

2. Use *awed* in a sentence about something you saw in a theater.

   _____

   _____

   _____

3. Describe a speech you heard. Use the word *anecdote* in your sentence.

   _____

   _____

   _____

4. Use *impromptu* in a sentence about something a friend did.

   _____

   _____

   _____

5. Describe something you did. Use *intently* in your sentence.

   _____

   _____

   _____

6. Use any form of the word *agonize* in a sentence about a problem you or someone you know encountered.

   _____

   _____

   _____

Each question below contains a vocabulary word from this lesson.
Answer each question "yes" or "no" in the space provided.

7. If you tear up some newspapers, do you leave it in *shrewds*?

7. _____

8. Could a music group be *cajoled* by an audience into playing certain songs?

8. _____

9. Can you *ensure* the weather will be sunny next week?

9. _____

10. Would you use an old *manuscript* to wash your car?

10. _____

For each question you answered "no," write a sentence explaining your reason.

_____

_____

_____

_____

_____

_____

_____

_____

_____

_____

_____

_____

Mastering Meaning

Describe a personal experience about a time when you had to perform before a group. Tell how you felt and what preparations you made to make the performance successful. Use some of the words you studied in this lesson.

Vocabulary of Anatomy

Name _____

Unlocking Meaning

The human body is filled with thousands of mechanisms and mysteries. There are words to describe each of these. Because the Greeks were the first to study anatomy systematically, many of the words for parts of the body come from their language. In this lesson, you will learn ten terms related to human anatomy.

Read the sentences or short passages below. Write the letter for the correct definition of the italicized vocabulary word.

Words

capillary

esophagus

larynx

lesion

ligament

marrow

metabolism

orthopedic

pulmonary

sinew

1. Jonas pricked the tip of his finger on a thumbtack. When the wound bled a little, he knew that he had punctured a *capillary*.
   (A) knuckle
   (B) tiny blood vessel
   (C) major blood vessel
   (D) wrist bone

2. The emergency crew was trained in the proper way to dislodge food caught in someone's *esophagus*.
   (A) facial muscles
   (B) mouth
   (C) tube connecting throat and stomach
   (D) tube connecting intestines and stomach

   1. _____

3. Because Kim had a minor infection of the *larynx,* her voice sounded husky.
   (A) lining of the stomach
   (B) part of the small intestine
   (C) chamber of the heart
   (D) part of the windpipe

   2. _____

4. When he fell off his bicycle, Ken suffered a serious *lesion* on his leg. At the hospital, a doctor cleaned and bandaged the wound.
   (A) lung disease
   (B) injury or abnormal change to tissues or organs
   (C) heart attack
   (D) tumor or other growth

   3. _____

   4. _____

5. During the soccer game, Jan extended her leg too far and strained a *ligament*. A tight bandage was needed to avoid further injury.
   (A) tough tissue that connects bones
   (B) soft tissue that lines the heart
   (C) one of several bones in the ankle
   (D) one of two major bones in the lower leg

   5. _____

6. The magnetic resonance imaging allowed the doctor to look beyond the bone and into the *marrow*.

6. _____

    (A) muscles and nerves
    (B) tough tissue that connects bones
    (C) soft tissue that fills the cavities of most bones
    (D) soft tissue that connects blood vessels

7. As his *metabolism* slowly increased, Julian began to lose weight. The doctor advised him that such changes were normal at his age.

7. _____

    (A) thoughts and feelings
    (B) social behavior
    (C) electrical currents that stimulate the heart
    (D) the body's process of turning food into energy

8. Kwan's fracture was more complicated than it first appeared. His family doctor referred him to an *orthopedic* surgeon.

8. _____

    (A) related to muscles
    (B) related to the eyes
    (C) related to bones
    (D) related to feet

9. Suddenly, Pierre's father had great difficulty breathing. At the hospital, he was diagnosed as having a *pulmonary* problem.

9. _____

    (A) related to the heart
    (B) related to the lungs
    (C) related to the ears
    (D) related to the pancreas

10. The runner had trained for months and it showed. As she leaned into the starting block, the *sinews* in her legs pulled her muscles so tightly that it reminded me of a rubber band stretched to the breaking point.

10. _____

    (A) blood vessels
    (B) glands that produce perspiration
    (C) tough tissues that connect muscles to bones
    (D) chemicals that aid in digestion

Applying Meaning

Rewrite each sentence. Replace the underlined word or words with a vocabulary word or a form of a vocabulary word.

1. When Anna fell, she skinned her knee and broke a few <u>small blood vessels</u>.

   _____

   _____

2. The first thing the emergency room doctor did was to press on my <u>tissue between bone and muscle</u>.

   _____

   _____

3. The doctor used a small light inside a magnifying glass to examine the <u>tube leading from my mouth to my stomach</u>.

   _____

   _____

4. Often one of the first signs of an allergy is the appearance of <u>abnormal changes</u> on the skin.

   _____

   _____

5. The air pollution was so severe that people with <u>lung</u> conditions were advised to stay indoors.

   _____

   _____

Each question below contains a vocabulary word from this lesson. Answer each question "yes" or "no" in the space provided.

6. Would you be wise to see an *orthopedic* doctor if you had a dislocated shoulder?

6. _____

7. If you injure your *larynx*, will eyeglasses help you?

7. _____

8. If your *metabolism* slows, are you likely to gain weight?

8. _____

9. Could a doctor examine your *marrow* with a magnifying glass?

9. _____

10. Could vigorous exercise strain a *ligament*?

10. _____

For each question you answered "no," write a sentence explaining your reason.

_____

_____

_____

_____

_____

_____

_____

_____

_____

_____

_____

_____

_____

_____

_____

_____

Our Living Language

The shapes and functions of the human body have been used as figures of speech to clarify or explain things that occur around us. The edge of a road is called the *shoulder* because its shape and position are similar to that of a human shoulder.

Explain the Figures of Speech: To what do each of the following figures of speech refer? Why is the human anatomy a good comparison?

eye of the storm   nose of the spacecraft   a neck of land

hairline fracture   lip of a pitcher

The Prefix *ad-*

Name _____

The Latin prefix *ad-* meaning "to" or "toward" appears in many forms. It is easy to see in a word like *admonish*, where *ad-* is added to the Latin root *monere*, meaning "to warn." However, when *ad-* appears before a word or root beginning with *c*, its spelling changes to *ac-*, and when it is used with a word beginning with *f*, its spelling changes to *af-*. Even so, the "to" or "toward" meaning is still part of the word in which it is found.

Prefix	Meaning	Word
ad-	to, toward	admonish
ad-	to, toward	accentuate
ad-	to, toward	affix

Unlocking Meaning

A vocabulary word appears in italics in each passage below. The meaning of the root is given in parentheses. Look at the prefix and think about how the word is used in the passage. Then write a definition for the vocabulary word. Compare your definition with the dictionary definition at the back of the book.

1. The cab drivers hoped their strike would *accentuate* the need to raise fares. (Root word: *cantus*, "song")

   _____

   _____

   _____

2. The general signaled his *acquiescence* to the terms of surrender with a nod of his head. (Root word: *quiescere*, "to rest")

   _____

   _____

   _____

3. The Rembrandt painting was the museum's most important *acquisition*. (Root word: *quaerere*, "to seek")

   _____

   _____

   _____

Words

accentuate

acquiescence

acquisition

admonish

advent

adversary

affiliate

affirm

affix

affliction

4. The counselor felt it necessary to *admonish* all campers to avoid eating any wild berries. (Root word: *monere*, "to warn")

_____

_____

_____

5. Before the *advent* of the computer, it took hours to prepare bank statements. (Root word: *vinire*, "to come")

_____

_____

_____

6. Because of his traitorous acts, Benedict Arnold became Washington's *adversary*. (Root word: *vertere*. "to turn")

_____

_____

_____

7. The minor league team hopes to *affiliate* with the New York Mets, a major league team. (Root word: *filius*, "son")

_____

_____

_____

8. I need a letter from the librarian to *affirm* that the fine has been paid. (Root word: *firmare*, "to strengthen")

_____

_____

_____

9. We were told to *affix* the beach sticker to the left corner of the windshield. (Root word: *figere*, "to fasten")

_____

_____

_____

10. The blind pianist was determined that his *affliction* would not halt his career. (Root word: *fligere*, "to strike")

_____

_____

_____

Name _____

Applying Meaning

Follow the directions below to write a sentence using a vocabulary word.

1. Describe an important turning point in history. Use the word *advent*.

   _____

   _____

   _____

2. Tell about something a parent or a teacher told you to do. Use any form of the word *admonish*.

   _____

   _____

   _____

3. Use any form of the word *affiliate* in a sentence about a club.

   _____

   _____

   _____

4. Use any form of the word *accentuate* in a sentence about an accident or a planned event.

   _____

   _____

   _____

Decide which word in parentheses best completes the sentence. Then write the sentence, adding the missing word.

5. The senator's opponent proved to be a fierce _____ in the first debate. (adversary; affliction)

   _____

   _____

   _____

6. After the luggage had been searched, a guard _____ tape to the lock and placed it on the plane. (affirmed; affixed)

   _____

   _____

   _____

7. Dad refused to take the job in Texas without the _____ of our entire family. (acquiescence; acquisition)

_____

_____

_____

8. Before the Salk vaccine, polio was a dreaded _____ for every family with children. (acquiescence; affliction)

_____

_____

_____

9. Don argued that the _____ of more weapons would not make the world safer. (acquiescence: acquisition)

_____

_____

_____

10. The courts have repeatedly _____ the right of every defendant to an attorney. (affirmed; affixed)

_____

_____

_____

Test-Taking Strategies

Tests of vocabulary sometimes ask you to choose a synonym for the word being tested. A synonym is a word with the <u>same or nearly the same</u> meaning. For example, *request* is a synonym for *ask*. When taking this type of test, you should study each choice and eliminate any answers that are clearly wrong.

Practice: Choose the synonym for the italicized word in each sentence. Write your choice on the answer line.

1. The senator's *scurrilous* attack on his opponent at the end of the debate came as a shock to everyone.
   (A) effective   (B) scholarly   (C) vulgar   (D) unreasonable

1. _____

2. A general *apathy* exists about recycling in many communities around this state.
   (A) hostility   (B) indifference   (C) sincerity   (D) confusion

2. _____

Name _____

How well do you remember the words you studied in Lessons 28 through 30? Take the following test covering the words from the last three lessons.

Part 1 Choose the Correct Meaning

Each question below includes a word in capital letters, followed by four words or phrases. Choose the word or phrase that is <u>closest</u> in meaning to the word in capital letters. Write the letter for your answer on the line provided.

Sample

S. FINISH	(A) enjoy (C) destroy	(B) complete (D) enlarge	S. ____**B**____

1. ENSURE	(A) guarantee (C) reply	(B) question (D) approve	1. _____
2. AFFILIATE	(A) make sick (C) associate with	(B) break from (D) surpass	2. _____
3. LESION	(A) severe pain (C) wound	(B) obstacle (D) bandage	3. _____
4. ADVERSARY	(A) supporter (C) teammate	(B) teacher (D) enemy	4. _____
5. IMPROMPTU	(A) heated (C) unrehearsed	(B) clever (D) brilliant	5. _____
6. CAPILLARY	(A) brain cell (C) organ	(B) nerve (D) blood vessel	6. _____
7. AFFIRM	(A) prove (C) order	(B) ask (D) debate	7. _____
8. EMINENT	(A) first (C) lucky	(B) well known (D) wealthy	8. _____
9. ADMONISH	(A) publicize (C) warn	(B) congratulate (D) forgive	9. _____
10. INTENTLY	(A) usually (C) secretly	(B) without interest (D) purposefully	10. _____

11. AFFLICTION (A) habit   (B) hardship   11. _____
         (C) good fortune (D) requirement

12. CAJOLE   (A) release   (B) demand   12. _____
         (C) coax   (D) bribe

13. ACQUIESCENCE (A) consent   (B) response   13. _____
         (C) dissent   (D) recognition

14. SHREWD   (A) forceful   (B) ineffective 14. _____
         (C) experienced (D) clever

15. AFFIX   (A) repair   (B) attach   15. _____
         (C) remove   (D) glue

Part 2 Matching Words and Meanings

Match the definition in Column B with the word in Column A. Write the letter of the correct definition on the line provided.

Column A   **Column B**

16. metabolism a. coming, arrival   16. _____

17. agonize   b. related to bones and joints   17. _____

18. pulmonary   c. soft tissue inside bones   18. _____

19. orthopedic   d. related to the lungs   19. _____

20. advent   e. suffer, struggle   20. _____

21. anecdote   f. a tale   21. _____

22. larynx   g. tissue that connects bones   22. _____

23. acquisition   h. the process of turning food into energy 23. _____

24. ligament   i. something gained or obtained 24. _____

25. marrow   j. part of the windpipe   25. _____

Name _____

The Statue of Liberty's Roots

On an island in New York Harbor stands a **prominent** symbol of the United States: the Statue of Liberty. This magnificent monument did not **originate** in the United States, however. The Statue of Liberty was a gift from the people of France to mark the one-hundred-year

5 anniversary of American independence. In 1869, sculptor Frédéric Auguste Bartholdi began to **execute** his concept for the monument.

Bartholdi chose the look of **classic** Greek and Roman figures. He envisioned Liberty as a strong and proud figure, one who **personified** not only the majestic Greek goddesses of the past,

10 but also the working men and women of the present. Liberty's mountainous **proportions** made it necessary for Bartholdi to first build a small plaster model of the huge statue that eventually would rise over 111 feet. The index finger alone had a span of 7 feet 11 inches.

15 Finally, in 1884, the work was finished, and Liberty was packed into 214 crates and sent to New York City. Only one problem stood in the way. While the French had raised $400,000 to build the statue, New York had not secured the funds to build its foundation. It was not until a New York newspaper **implored** people

20 for donations that money became available. Boys and girls sent spare change. Small donations by the thousands began to pour in. Finally, there was enough money to build the foundation, and on October 28, 1886, Americans celebrated the unveiling of the Statue of Liberty.

25 In the years that followed, the Statue of Liberty welcomed thousands of immigrants. In the 1980s, when the statue was found to have serious structural problems, people again rallied to restore the weak structure and **refurbish** the tarnished monument. During a full-scale **restoration**, the iron skeleton was reinforced with

30 300,000 additional rivets and painted a bright **vermilion** red to preserve the finish. Then Liberty was once again covered with copper. Today, the Statue of Liberty continues to stand as a symbol of freedom for those arriving on the United States' shores.

Words

classic

execute

implore

originate

personified

prominent

proportion

refurbish

restoration

vermilion

Each word in this lesson's word list appears in dark type in the selection you just read. Think about how the vocabulary word is used in the selection, then write the letter for the best answer to each question.

1. Another word for *prominent* in line 1 is _____.
   (A) victorious   (B) noticeable
   (C) wholesome   (D) secluded

1. _____

2. Which word or words could best replace *originate* in line 3?
   (A) become rejected   (B) lose its way
   (C) expand   (D) come into being

2. _____

3. If you *execute* (line 6) a plan, you _____.
   (A) carry it out   (B) assign it to others
   (C) destroy it completely   (D) revise it

3. _____

4. A *classic* (line 7) figure is _____.
   (A) expensive   (B) difficult to understand
   (C) a model example   (D) simple

4. _____

5. If something is *personified* (line 9), it is _____.
   (A) falsely taken   (B) used as an example
   (C) never realized   (D) hopeless

5. _____

6. *Proportions* (line 11) refers to _____.
   (A) color and length (B) artistic impression
   (C) dimension and size   (D) weight and texture

6. _____

7. Another word for *implored* (line 19) is _____.
   (A) begged   (B) taxed
   (C) threatened   (D) gestured

7. _____

8. If you *refurbish* (line 28) something, you _____.
   (A) build an addition to it   (B) take its measurements
   (C) make it fresh and bright again   (D) replace it

8. _____

9. *Restoration* in line 29 is _____.
   (A) the act of paying for a project   (B) a type of dedication
   (C) the act of creating a duplicate   (D) the act of bringing back to original condition

9. _____

10. When something is given a coat of *vermilion* paint (line 30), it becomes _____.
    (A) bright red   (B) black
    (C) warm   (D) rusted

10. _____

Applying Meaning

Read each sentence below. Write "correct" on the answer line if the vocabulary word has been used correctly or "incorrect" if it has been used incorrectly.

1. The large fountain was the most *prominent* feature of the garden.

2. Since it was Josh's birthday, the biggest *proportion* of the cake was given to him.

3. For her second dive, Lil planned to *execute* a twisting two-and-a-half somersault.

4. The candidate *implored* his supporters to donate their time and money.

5. Jazz is said to have *originated* in New Orleans, but other cities also claim it.

6. We were told that any scraps of food left lying around would attract *vermilion*.

1. _____

2. _____

3. _____

4. _____

5. _____

6. _____

For each word used incorrectly, write a sentence using the word properly.

_____

_____

_____

_____

_____

_____

_____

_____

_____

_____

_____

Follow the directions below to write a sentence using a vocabulary word.

7. Describe a car or a piece of music. Use the word *classic* in your sentence.

_____

_____

_____

8. Write a sentence about an old building. Use any form of the word *restoration*.

_____

_____

_____

9. Use *personified* in a sentence about a quality such as honesty or self-sacrifice.

_____

_____

_____

10. Use *refurbish* in a sentence about a project you or someone you know undertook recently.

_____

_____

_____

Mastering Meaning

Twenty-five hundred people stood on Bedloe's Island in New York City on October 28, 1886, as the Statue of Liberty was unveiled. President Cleveland was the last of several speakers to address the audience. Write a short speech you would have liked to deliver on this occasion. Use some of the words you studied in this lesson.

Name _____

Unlocking Meaning

In describing the appearance or condition of something, words like *good*, *bad*, *nice*, and *pretty* do not tell you very much. In this lesson, you will learn ten adjectives that give a more exact description of the physical appearance or condition of people, places, or objects

Read the sentences or short passages below. Write the letter for the correct definition of the italicized vocabulary word.

Words
blighted
comely
decrepit
drab
lackluster
mundane
pallid
radiant
resplendent
slovenly

1. Because of the heat spell and a lack of rain, the lettuce in the garden had a *blighted* appearance.
   (A) ripe
   (B) soggy or wet
   (C) withered and ruined
   (D) light green

2. Everyone at the party complimented Janet on her new, *comely* hairstyle.
   (A) unattractive
   (B) attractive
   (C) stringy
   (D) difficult to manage

3. Ms. Talarvan's friends were concerned when she bought the old, *decrepit* house. A year later, they were impressed when they saw the improvements she had made.
   (A) wooden
   (B) stone or brick
   (C) inexpensive
   (D) broken down or worn-out

4. Sherry and her father repainted the walls of her bedroom. Once *drab* and dark, the room now seemed bright and cheerful.
   (A) dull and faded
   (B) hidden
   (C) small and insignificant
   (D) untidy

5. Herb's *lackluster* speech and monotonous tone of voice put most of the audience to sleep.
   (A) interesting and fun
   (B) easy
   (C) boring or unimaginative
   (D) too difficult

6. We had hoped the business course would address the obligations of employer and employee. Instead, it was the same *mundane* study of inventory, finance, and marketing.
   (A) longer
   (B) noisy
   (C) restful
   (D) ordinary or common

1. _____

2. _____

3. _____

4. _____

5. _____

6. _____

7. Although he was not injured, Pete had a *pallid* appearance after
   the accident. The doctor decided to keep him under observation
   until the blood returned to his face.
   (A) pale   (B) untidy
   (C) bruised   (D) scratched

   7. _____

8. I felt strange and lonely in the new school until Beth introduced
   herself and flashed her *radiant,* friendly smile.
   (A) shy   (B) bright and shiny
   (C) sly or clever   (D) humorous

   8. _____

9. The parade float was a *resplendent* display of yellow and red
   flowers, colorful streamers, and costumed performers.
   (A) dazzling; beautiful   (B) ordinary; common
   (C) interesting   (D) creative

   9. _____

10. When I crossed out several lines in my composition, I tore the
    corner of the paper. The teacher refused to accept such *slovenly*
    work, so I had to make a clean copy.
    (A) unfashionable   (B) tired and disappointed
    (C) sloppy or careless (D) filled with light

    10. _____

Applying Meaning

Each question below contains a vocabulary word from this lesson.
Answer each question "yes" or "no" in the space provided.

1. Would a person with a *slovenly* appearance make a good impression in a job interview?   1. _____

2. Would a neighborhood organization work to achieve a *blighted*   2. _____
   community?

3. Are *drab* colors appropriate for funerals and other sad occasions?   3. _____

4. Would a day in the sun leave you with a *pallid* appearance?   4. _____

5. Would yellow walls and numerous windows make a room *radiant*   5. _____
   on a sunny day?

For each question you answered "no," write a sentence explaining
your reason.

_____

_____

_____

_____

_____

_____

_____

_____

Decide which word in parentheses best completes the sentence. Then
write the sentence, adding the missing word.

6. The store's Christmas tree was _____ with twinkling lights and silver
   ornaments. (lackluster; resplendent)

   _____

   _____

   _____

7. Fred planned the banquet, but left the _____ task of addressing the
   envelopes to his assistant. (comely; mundane)

   _____

   _____

   _____

8. After paying $500 to rent the cottage, we were unhappy with its
   _____ appearance when we saw it. (decrepit; pallid)

   _____

   _____

   _____

9. The little girl's _____ smile delighted her grandfather. (comely; drab)

   _____

   _____

   _____

10. In spite of the actor's _____ performance as Lincoln, Frieda
    planned to see him in another role. (lackluster; resplendent)

    _____

    _____

    _____

Spelling and Meaning

the boy's hat   the workers' uniforms   the mice's food

The possessive form of a noun shows ownership. A singular noun like
boy requires an apostrophe (') and *s*: the boy's hat. Plural nouns ending
in *s* require only an apostrophe: the workers' uniforms. Other plural
nouns, like *mice* and *women* require both an apostrophe and *s*: the
mice's food, the women's locker.

Change each of these nouns into a possessive noun. Then write a
sentence using each possessive noun correctly.

Jess   children   Tony   girls   bus   geese   wolves

Noun Suffixes

Name _____

The *-ion, -tion* and *-sion* suffixes are used to change verbs into nouns. Sometimes the suffix is simply added to the verb, but often the spelling is also changed in other ways. Study the examples below.

Verb	Suffix	Noun
ignite	-ion	ignition
emit	-sion	emission
reform	-tion	reformation

Unlocking Meaning

A vocabulary word appears in italics in each sentence or short passage below. Think about the verb and noun forms of the word. Then write a definition for the vocabulary word. Compare your definition with the definition in the dictionary at the back of the book.

1. The coach will designate the starting quarterback today. His *designation* will be watched anxiously by all the players.

   _____

   _____

   _____

2. The factory emits pollution into the air. The governor insisted that these *emissions* stop.

   _____

   _____

   _____

3. The astronauts must ignite their rockets. This *ignition* positions the craft for a safe return to earth.

   _____

   _____

   _____

4. The club will induct its new members at the next meeting. The *induction* ceremony will be held in the hotel ballroom.

   _____

   _____

   _____

Words

- designation
- emission
- ignition
- induction
- inversion
- liberation
- provision
- recession
- recuperation
- reformation

5. I inverted the vase to see if it had been signed by its maker. The *inversion* caused a piece of paper to fall out.

_____

_____

_____

6. The victorious army liberated the prisoners. The *liberation* was a cause for great celebration.

_____

_____

_____

7. The outfitters will provide maps and flashlights for our hike in the cave. These *provisions* are essential for safety.

_____

_____

_____

8. It took weeks for the floodwaters to recede. Even after the waters' *recession*, it took months to clean up the mud.

_____

_____

_____

9. The doctor felt Floyd should recuperate in the hospital. Without this *recuperation*, the illness might return.

_____

_____

_____

10. The prisoner promised he would reform his behavior. The judge doubted that such a *reformation* was possible.

_____

_____

_____

Applying Meaning

Follow the directions below to write a sentence using a vocabulary word.

1. Tell about a hiking trip you might take. Use any form of the word *provision*.

_____

_____

_____

2. Describe an important change an individual or a group made. Use the word *reformation*.

_____

_____

_____

3. Write a sentence about a historic event. Use the word *liberation*.

_____

_____

_____

4. Describe an important decision. Use the word *designation*.

_____

_____

_____

5. Use the word *ignition* in a sentence about an accident.

_____

_____

_____

Decide which word in parentheses best completes the sentence. Then write the sentence, adding the missing word.

6. The injured player's _____ was slow and painful because of his earlier injuries. (recession; recuperation)

_____

_____

_____

7. The trick mirror turned everything upside down. This _____ both confused and amused the guests. (inversion; recession)

_____

_____

_____

8. The chemical plant's high _____ levels of sulfur fumes caused its neighbors to complain. (emission; induction)

_____

_____

_____

9. The mayor's _____ into office was applauded by his supporters, who had worked diligently to get him elected. (induction; inversion)

_____

_____

_____

10. The _____ in economic activity soon resulted in the loss of jobs. (recession; provision)

_____

_____

_____

Cultural Literacy Note

One of the oddities of English is the palindrome—a word, phrase, or sentence that reads the same backward or forward. The simplest palindromes are words in a consonant-vowel-consonant pattern like *dad* or *pop,* but there are many longer words that work as well, such as *radar* and *level.* Some sentence palindromes can be several words long, such as "A man, a plan, a canal, Panama!"

Cooperative Learning: With a partner, brainstorm a list of word and sentence palindromes.

How well do you remember the words you studied in Lessons 31 through 33? Take the following test covering the words from the last three lessons.

Part 1 Choose the Correct Meaning

Each question below includes a word in capital letters, followed by four words or phrases. Choose the word or phrase that is <u>closest</u> in meaning to the word in capital letters. Write the letter for your answer on the line provided.

Sample

S. FINISH	(A) enjoy (C) destroy	(B) complete (D) enlarge	S. ___**B**___
1. PROVISIONS	(A) food (C) tools	(B) camping gear (D) supplies	1. _____
2. ORIGINATE	(A) verify the origin (C) cultivate	(B) grow (D) begin	2. _____
3. PALLID	(A) unpleasant (C) yellow	(B) colorless (D) ruddy	3. _____
4. DESIGNATION	(A) intention (C) selection	(B) substitute (D) subordinate	4. _____
5. IMPLORE	(A) beg (C) order	(B) investigate (D) forbid	5. _____
6. RECUPERATION	(A) recovery (C) advise	(B) attention (D) medication	6. _____
7. SLOVENLY	(A) hasty (C) poor	(B) sloppy (D) illegible	7. _____
8. PROMINENT	(A) noticeable (C) unchanging	(B) promising (D) solid	8. _____
9. RESPLENDENT	(A) expensive (C) dazzling	(B) complicated (D) detailed	9. _____
10. PERSONIFIED	(A) maligned (C) celebrated	(B) embodied (D) copied	10. _____

11. INDUCTION   (A) lessening   (B) conclusion   11. _____
                     (C) preface   (D) initiation

12. DECREPIT   (A) run-down   (B) old   12. _____
                    (C) dirty   (D) colonial

13. MUNDANE   (A) ordinary   (B) stupid   13. _____
                   (C) difficult   (D) old-fashioned

14. REFORMATION   (A) change   (B) improvement   14. _____
                      (C) religious belief   (D) promise

15. EXECUTE   (A) modify   (B) supervise   15. _____
                  (C) carry out   (D) review

Part 2 Matching Words and Meanings

Match the definition in Column B with the word in Column A. Write
the letter of the correct definition on the line provided.

Column A	Column B	
16. proportion	a. brilliant	16. _____
17. emission	b. size and dimension	17. _____
18. recession	c. unimaginative	18. _____
19. blighted	d. pretty	19. _____
20. vermilion	e. ruined	20. _____
21. radiant	f. output	21. _____
22. liberation	g. act of setting on fire	22. _____
23. ignition	h. withdrawing	23. _____
24. lackluster	i. bright red	24. _____
25. comely	j. freeing	25. _____

Name _____

Fossils Trapped in Tar

Not far from the **congestion** of the Los Angeles freeways, saber-tooth cats, mastodons, and giant ground sloths once roamed the land. During the Ice Age, which **encompassed** a period of time some 10,000 to 40,000 years ago, over 400 different kinds of
5   animals lived on the grassy plain that is now Los Angeles.

Then, as now, large deposits of oil lay beneath the earth in California. When these deposits seeped through the cracks in the surface, the oil evaporated, leaving pools of sticky tar that would catch leaves and other forms of ground cover. During
10 colder weather, these pools **congealed**, trapping the leaves in the hardened tar. Then in the summer heat the tar pools beneath the leaves softened into an ooze similar to molasses. Unsuspecting animals walked into the ooze and sank. Once these beasts became **immersed** in the tar, it was nearly impossible for them to escape.
15 These oily tar pits caused the **demise** of thousands of animals. The animals' remains did not vanish, however. The same tar that caused their deaths also **pervaded** their bones and preserved them as fossils.

Until 1906, the tar from Rancho La Brea was **excavated** for use
20 as a glue. It was then that Dr. John C. Merriam, at the University of California, realized the importance of the fossils that were being dug up along with the tar. After that, scientists began the **fervid** excavation of these revealing fossils. Evidence of mammoths, mastodons, saber-tooth cats, lions, wolves, sloths, camels, horses,
25 and other animals was uncovered.

In 1977 the fossils were placed in a museum and research center. There paleontologists study bone fossils, which tell of events that took place thousands of years ago, and try to explain why the animals became extinct. One theory is that they were overhunted
30 by early humans. While it is difficult to **confute** this theory, some scientists question why the bones of only one human have been found in the Rancho La Brea tar pits. As scientists continue to **probe** for answers, their discoveries about the past may help us glimpse the future.

Words
confute
congeal
congestion
demise
encompass
excavate
fervid
immerse
pervade
probe

Each word in this lesson's word list appears in dark type in the selection you just read. Think about how the vocabulary word is used in the selection, then write the letter for the best answer to each question.

1. *Congestion* (line 1) means _____.
   (A) overcrowding   (B) disharmony
   (C) danger   (D) scenic views

   1. _____

2. If you *encompass* something, (line 3) you _____.
   (A) explain it   (B) ignore it
   (C) include it   (D) change it

   2. _____

3. To *congeal* (line 10) is to _____.
   (A) thicken   (B) pass over
   (C) reverse direction   (D) guard

   3. _____

4. Which word or words could best replace *immersed* in line 14?
   (A) thirsty   (B) completely covered
   (C) broken   (D) displayed

   4. _____

5. Another word for *demise* in line 15 is _____.
   (A) sickness   (B) burden
   (C) difficulty   (D) death

   5. _____

6. *Pervaded* in line 17 means _____.
   (A) released   (B) spread throughout
   (C) cured   (D) destroyed

   6. _____

7. Which words could best replace *excavated* in line 19?
   (A) upset the natural balance   (B) uncovered by digging
   (C) tore up the landscape   (D) buried by digging

   7. _____

8. Another word for *fervid* (line 22) is _____.
   (A) casual   (B) enthusiastic
   (C) humorous   (D) unscientific

   8. _____

9. If you *confute* (line 30) a theory, you _____.
   (A) disprove it   (B) prove it conclusively
   (C) explain it   (D) ridicule it

   9. _____

10. Another word for *probe* (line 33) is _____.
    (A) pitch   (B) mention
    (C) test   (D) explore

    10. _____

Applying Meaning

Decide which word in parentheses best completes the sentence. Then write the sentence, adding the missing word.

1. The photographer _____ the film in a liquid developing fluid. (probed; immersed)

   _____

   _____

   _____

2. The reckless driver caused the _____ of four innocent victims. (congestion: demise)

   _____

   _____

   _____

3. To complete the road, engineers had to _____ a tunnel through a mountain. (encompass: excavate)

   _____

   _____

   _____

4. Overnight the melted ice cream on the kitchen floor began to _____ (confute; congeal)

   _____

   _____

   _____

5. After the final count was announced, a stunned silence _____ the losing candidate's headquarters. (pervaded; probed)

   _____

   _____

   _____

Follow the directions below to write a sentence using a vocabulary word.

6. Describe an argument. Use any form of the word *confute*.

_____

_____

_____

7. Write a sentence about an investigation. Use the word *probe*.

_____

_____

_____

8. Write a sentence about something you want. Use any form of the word *fervid*.

_____

_____

_____

9. Use *congestion* in a sentence about your school.

_____

_____

_____

10. Use any form of the word *encompass* in a sentence about a report.

_____

_____

_____

Mastering Meaning

Imagine that you are a paleontologist applying for a job at the museum that houses the Rancho La Brea fossils. Write a letter expressing why you think the museum's research is important and what contribution you could make to the work being done there. Use some of the words you studied in this lesson.

Vocabulary of Speech and Expression

Lesson
35
Part A

Name _____

Unlocking Meaning

There are probably hundreds of ways to say simple words like *yes* and *no*. Your tone of voice, gestures, or facial expressions flavor the words you say. In this lesson, you will learn ten words that flavor the many ways we speak and communicate our individual feelings to others.

Read the sentences or short passages below. Write the letter for the correct definition of the italicized vocabulary word.

Words
banter
beseech
bicker
blasphemy
coerce
lampoon
reiterate
scathing
scoff
scorn

1. On my favorite comedy show, the host often engages his guests in some entertaining, good-natured *banter* to get a few laughs.
   (A) conversation involving questions
   (B) conversation involving critical analysis
   (C) discussion of current events
   (D) playful conversation

2. When the citizens realized their town was surrounded by enemy troops, they decided to *beseech* friendly countries for assistance.
   (A) demand loudly
   (B) plead or request in a serious way
   (C) shyly suggest
   (D) ask in a casual or leisurely way

   1. _____

3. My two little brothers sometimes tire me out! They *bicker* about really silly things, such as whose turn it is to turn off their bedside lamp.
   (A) to talk quietly, watching one's words and tone of voice
   (B) to make jokes about; ridicule
   (C) to quarrel or squabble over unimportant matters
   (D) to suggest compromises

   2. _____

   3. _____

4. The vandals defaced and destroyed many of the monuments in the veterans' cemetery. Such *blasphemy* should not go unpunished.
   (A) show of respect
   (B) falsehood that is repeated many times
   (C) attempt to express one's self
   (D) act of disrespect toward something sacred

   4. _____

   5. _____

5. By threatening to move the team to another city, the owners were just trying to *coerce* the city into building a new stadium.
   (A) humor someone into agreeing with you
   (B) persuade though power or threats
   (C) prevent by law
   (D) suggest gently

6. The movie's script was a *lampoon* of all the so-called action movies. The audience roared at the unbelievable events and pointless explosions that unfolded in slow motion on the screen.
   (A) type of humor based on exaggeration
   (B) writing based on careful thought and analysis
   (C) type of compliment
   (D) writing that attempts to persuade people

6. _____

7. Because several students were having difficulty deciding what to do, the teacher decided to *reiterate* the directions.
   (A) change
   (B) repeat
   (C) shout or chant
   (D) murmur

7. _____

8. The committee members issued a *scathing* report blaming the supervisor for the accident that injured several workers.
   (A) complimentary
   (B) ridiculous
   (C) severely critical
   (D) complicated

8. _____

9. The boaters were foolish to *scoff* at the Coast Guard's warning about the oncoming storm.
   (A) dismiss or mock as unimportant
   (B) believe completely
   (C) persuade others to listen
   (D) attack forcefully

9. _____

10. His friends ridiculed Ed's decision to start his own business, so he was right to *scorn* their efforts to make up to him when he became successful.
    (A) respect
    (B) confuse and puzzle
    (C) show sympathy or concern
    (D) reject or refuse

10. _____

Applying Meaning

Decide which word in parentheses best completes the sentence. Then write the sentence, adding the missing word.

1. After listening to the children _____ over who got the larger dessert, I decided to leave the table. (bicker; scoff)

   _____

   _____

   _____

2. The police felt it was important to _____ the warning about the escaped prisoner. (beseech; reiterate)

   _____

   _____

   _____

3. The president made a _____ speech accusing the terrorists of attacking innocent people. (coercing; scathing)

   _____

   _____

   _____

4. Even though Barbara was anxious to sell the car, she _____ at the amount we offered for it. (lampooned; scoffed)

   _____

   _____

   _____

5. By threatening to fire them, the director hoped to _____ the strikers into returning to their jobs. (banter; coerce)

   _____

   _____

   _____

6. The tearful woman _____ the person who took her dog to return it. (beseeched; coerced)

   _____

   _____

7. Criticizing the local baseball team is almost considered a form of
_____ in this sports-crazy town. (blasphemy; lampoon)

_____

_____

_____

8. Some of the silly _____ between comics like Abbott and Costello is
considered classic. (banter; scorn)

_____

_____

_____

9. The editor of the humor magazine included a _____ of a local
politician in every issue. (blasphemy; lampoon)

_____

_____

_____

10. In the fairy tale, the evil king treated his subjects with _____, refusing
even to meet with them. (scorn; lampoon)

_____

_____

_____

Using the Dictionary

Homographs

Two or more words that are spelled the same way, but have different

meanings and origins are called *homographs*. Each homograph has its

own numbered entry in a dictionary. Even though the words look and

sound the same, they are, in fact, different words.

bay^1 (bā) *n.* a body of water partly enclosed by land.

bay^2 (bā) *n.* a type of window.

bay^3 (bā) *n.* a reddish-brown horse.

bay^4 (bā) *n.* a long howl or bark.

Use a classroom dictionary to find the definitions for these homographs:

bark; maroon; converse; file

Adjective Suffixes

Name _____

Certain endings are used to change the way a word is used in a sentence. One such ending is the adjective suffix. An adjective suffix is used to change a word from a naming word, or noun, to a describing word, or adjective. Note how the suffixes below change the way the words are used in sentences.

Noun	Adjective Suffix	Adjective
geometry	-ic	geometric
influence	-ial	influential
larceny	-ous	larcenous
maniac	-al	maniacal

Words

geometric

influential

larcenous

lecherous

maniacal

medicinal

metallic

parasitic

strenuous

synonymous

Unlocking Meaning

A vocabulary word appears in italics in each sentence or short passage below. Choose the letter for the correct definition of the italicized word. Write the letter for your answer on the line provided.

1. Geometry is my favorite class. I love studying the various *geometric* shapes and the ways in which they are created.
   (A) related to the characteristics and measurements of lines and figures
   (B) having to do with rocks and minerals
   (C) invisible
   (D) formed in ancient times

   1. _____

2. The newspaper was very *influential* in the last election. Some even feel its influence changed the outcome of the vote.
   (A) well informed
   (B) having the ability to increase in size
   (C) not easily bent
   (D) having the power to change an event

   2. _____

3. The judge wondered if, after his third conviction, the thief's *larcenous* behavior could ever be changed.
   (A) characterized by rude behavior
   (B) involving theft
   (C) lacking truth
   (D) exceptional

   3. _____

4. The early settlers sometimes punished *lecherous* behavior by publicly humiliating the offenders.
   (A) talkative
   (B) lewd
   (C) reverent
   (D) revolutionary

   4. _____

5. The fullback charged into the line like a maniac, knocking down every player in his path. His *maniacal* behavior even frightened his coach.

5. _____

(A) mad
(B) clever
(C) heroic
(D) pleasing

6. We rarely think of garlic as a medicine. However, some claim that garlic has a *medicinal* effect on high blood pressure and other illnesses.

6. _____

(A) exotic or foreign in nature
(B) spiritual
(C) having the ability to treat a disease
(D) harmful

7. As the water passed through the metal pipes, it took on a rather bitter, *metallic* taste.

7. _____

(A) having the characteristics of a disease
(B) having a sweet flavor
(C) having to do with meteors
(D) having the qualities of lead, copper, iron, and similar elements

8. Only a parasite would expect his parents to support him after he leaves school and gets a good job. I know my parents would never allow such *parasitic* behavior.

8. _____

(A) generous
(B) thoughtful about others
(C) tending to live off others
(D) discourteous and selfish

9. It is important that I not strain the damaged muscles in my leg, so my doctor advised me to avoid all *strenuous* activity for a while.

9. _____

(A) requiring great energy
(B) disorganized
(C) carefully planned
(D) unusual

10. The answer key to the test gave *stout* as a synonym for *fat*. Personally, I do not think they are at all *synonymous*.

10. _____

(A) having the opposite meaning
(B) having the same meaning
(C) correctly identified
(D) rhythmical

Applying Meaning

Decide which word in parentheses best completes the sentence. Then write the sentence, adding the missing word.

1. After Benedict Arnold betrayed his country to the British, his name became _____ with *traitor*. (larcenous; synonymous)

   _____

   _____

   _____

2. The plastic had become so hard that it began to take on certain _____ properties. (medicinal; metallic)

   _____

   _____

   _____

3. Many patterns in early quilts consist of circles, squares, and similar _____ figures. (geometric; parasitic)

   _____

   _____

   _____

4. The police vowed to arrest those _____ drivers who race through town blowing their horns. (lecherous; maniacal)

   _____

   _____

   _____

5. Because the job was _____ and involved heavy lifting, all employees were required to pass a physical examination. (influential; strenuous)

   _____

   _____

   _____

6. The officer's behavior was _____. (lecherous; medicinal)

   _____

   _____

   _____

Follow the directions below to write a sentence using a vocabulary word.

7. Describe someone you know or have read about. Use the word *influential*.

_____

_____

_____

8. Describe the relationship between two people. Use the word *parasitic*.

_____

_____

_____

9. Use *larcenous* in a sentence about something you feel is wrong.

_____

_____

_____

10. Tell about something that you find refreshing. Use the word *medicinal*.

_____

_____

_____

Test-Taking Strategies

Tests of reading comprehension ask you to read one or two selections and answer some questions to test how well you understood what you read. The questions often ask you to draw inferences from the information. For example, if the selection described someone wiping sweat off his face, you would be expected to infer that he is hot.

Practice: Reread the selection "Tropical Rain Forests" on page 113. Write an X next to the statements that might be inferred from this essay.

1. It is dangerous to walk in tropical rain forests. 1. _____

2. Animals in the rain forest have adapted to their surroundings. 2. _____

3. Human beings cannot survive in a tropical rain forest. 3. _____

4. When rain forests are destroyed animals lose their natural habitat. 4. _____

Name _____

How well do you remember the words you studied in Lessons 33 through 36? Take the following test covering the words from the last three lessons.

Part 1 Choose the Correct Meaning

Each question below includes a word in capital letters, followed by four words or phrases. Choose the word or phrase that is <u>closest</u> in meaning to the word in capital letters. Write the letter for your answer on the line provided.

Sample

S. FINISH	(A) enjoy	(B) complete	S. _____**B**_____
	(C) destroy	(D) enlarge	

1. EXCAVATE	(A) escape	(B) dig out	1. _____
	(C) explore	(D) study	
2. LAMPOON	(A) type of weapon	(B) part of a lamp	2. _____
	(C) insult	(D) ridicule	
3. INFLUENTIAL	(A) source of disease	(B) powerful	3. _____
	(C) corrupt	(D) pleasing	
4. PARASITIC	(A) living off others	(B) spiritual	4. _____
	(C) generous	(D) tending to spoil easily	
5. STRENUOUS	(A) heroic	(B) strict	5. _____
	(C) energetic	(D) eager	
6. SCOFF	(A) scrape	(B) raise up	6. _____
	(C) mock	(D) prove	
7. FERVID	(A) heated	(B) unusual	7. _____
	(C) reverent	(D) eager	
8. DEMISE	(A) death	(B) device	8. _____
	(C) type of tool	(D) unit of measurement	
9. BANTER	(A) argument	(B) chatter	9. _____
	(C) facial expression	(D) religious belief	
10. MANIACAL	(A) entertaining	(B) illegal	10. _____
	(C) insane	(D) manly	

11. SYNONYMOUS   (A) spicy   (B) simple   11. _____

                      (C) having the opposite   (D) having the same
                             meaning   meaning

12. COERCE   (A) join together   (B) compel   12. _____

                      (C) destroy   (D) beg

13. IMMERSE   (A) cover   (B) enlarge   13. _____

                      (C) copy   (D) doubt

14. PERVADE   (A) persuade   (B) delay   14. _____

                      (C) attack   (D) sink in

15. REITERATE   (A) engrave   (B) identify   15. _____

                      (C) restate   (D) ignore

Part 2 Matching Words and Meaning

Match the definition in Column B with the word in Column A. Write
the letter of the correct definition on the answer line.

Column A	Column B	
16. confute	a. involving theft	16. _____
17. beseech	b. extremely critical	17. _____
18. larcenous	c. thickness	18. _____
19. scorn	d. prove to be wrong	19. _____
20. congeal	e. healing	20. _____
21. medicinal	f. plead	21. _____
22. bicker	g. encircle	22. _____
23. scathing	h. harden	23. _____
24. congestion	i. squabble	24. _____
25. encompass	j. reject	25. _____

Dictionary

Pronunciation Guide

Symbol	Example	Symbol	Example
ă	p**a**t	oi	b**oy**
ā	p**ay**	ou	**out**
âr	c**are**	ŏŏ	t**oo**k
ä	f**a**ther	ōō	b**oo**t
ĕ	p**e**t	ŭ	c**u**t
ē	b**e**	ûr	**ur**ge
ĭ	p**i**t	th	**th**in
ī	p**ie**	*th*	**th**is
îr	p**ier**	hw	**wh**ich
ŏ	p**o**t	zh	vi**s**ion
ō	t**oe**	ə	**a**bout, item
ô	p**aw**		

Stress Marks: ′(primary); ′(secondary), as in **dictionary** (dĭk′shə-nĕr′ē)

A

ab·di·cate (ăb′dĭ kāt′) *v.* **ab·di·cat·ed, ab·di·cat·ing, ab·di·cates.** To formally give up (power, responsibility, or rights): *The elderly queen abdicated her throne to her son.*

ab·hor (ăb hôr′) *v.* **ab·horred, ab·hor·ring, ab·hors.** To feel hatred or disgust for; detest; loathe: *I abhor ticks and mosquitoes.*

ab·hor·rent (ăb **hôr**′ənt *or* ăb **hŏr**′ənt) *adj.* Causing disgust or hatred; horrible; detestable: *The abhorrent crime shocked us.*

a·bom·i·na·tion (ə bŏm′ə **nā**′shən) *n.* **1.** A feeling of disgust or hatred. **2.** Something that is disgusting or hateful: *Deliberately setting a forest fire is an abomination.*

ab·o·rig·i·ne (ăb′ə rĭj′ə nē) *n.* One of the first known people to have lived in a region or country: *The aborigines were able to survive without modern conveniences.*

a·bort (ə bôrt′) *v.* To end something before it is completed: *The scientists aborted the rocket launch because of bad weather.*

a·bound (ə bound′) *v.* To exist or be available in large numbers; plentiful: *Wildlife abounds in the national forests.*

ab·ra·sive (ə brā′sĭv *or* ə brā′zĭv) *adj.* **1.** Causing a wearing away or rubbing off: *The abrasive cleanser harmed the wood table.* **2.** Irritating in manner. —*n.* A substance such as sandpaper used for polishing, cleaning, or grinding. —**a·bra′sive·ly** *adv.* —**a·bra′sive·ness** *n.*

a·brupt (ə brŭpt′) *adj.* **1.** Happening suddenly or unexpectedly: *The abrupt change in the flight schedule upset the travelers.* **2.** Steep. **3.** Blunt; impolite. —**a·brupt′ly** *adv.* —**a·brupt′ness** *n.*

ab·so·lute (ăb′sə lōōt′) *adj.* **1.** Complete or perfect: *The witness told the absolute truth.* **2.** Not restricted or limited: *The government was based on absolute freedom for the citizens.* **3.** Not doubted; utter: *The mother's love was absolute.*

ab·stain (ăb stān′) *v.* To voluntarily keep oneself from doing something: *I abstain from eating foods that are high in fat.*

a·buse (ə byōōz′) *v.* **a·bused, a·bus·ing, a·bus·es. 1.** To use improperly or wrongly; misuse: *The mother told her children not to abuse their telephone privileges.* **2.** Mistreat; injure: *The dog owner was arrested for abusing the dog.* **3.** To attack or insult with harsh words. —*n.* (ə byōōs′) Misuse: *Drug abuse is illegal.*

ac·cen·tu·ate (ăk sĕn′chōō āt′) *v.* **ac·cen·tu·at·ed, ac·cen·tu·at·ing, ac·cen·tu·ates.** To emphasize; stress: *The earrings accentuate the woman's blue eyes.*

ac·co·lade (ăk′ə lād′ *or* ăk′ə läd′) *n.* An expression of approval such as praise, an award, or honor: *The astronaut was given accolades for his work in space.*

ac·com·plished (ə kŏm′plĭsht) *adj.* Skilled; expert: *The lifeguard is an accomplished swimmer.* *v.* Successfully carried out; completed: *The girl accomplished her reading goal.*

ac·qui·es·cence (ăk′wē ĕs′əns) *n.* Quiet agreement without protest: *The teacher was surprised by the students' acquiescence to the new rules.*

ac·qui·si·tion (ăk′wĭ zĭsh′ən) *n.* **1.** The act of obtaining or getting: *The students were thrilled about the school's acquisition of new computers.* **2.** Something acquired: *The rare bird is the zoo's newest acquisition.*

ad·den·dum (ə dĕn′dəm) *n., pl.* **ad·den·da.** Something that is added; addition: *Movies about real people often have an addendum at the end to explain what became of the people.*

ad·mon·ish (ăd mŏn′ĭsh) *v.* **1.** To warn or caution against something: *The health department admonished consumers not to eat raw meat.* **2.** To scold or criticize in a mild way: *The teacher admonished us for whispering during the assembly.* **—ad·mon′ish·ment** *n.*

ad·vent (ăd′vĕnt′) *n.* The arrival or coming into being of a new thing or person: *The advent of cellular telephones allowed people to make calls from almost anywhere.*

ad·ver·sar·y (ăd′vər sĕr′ē) *n., pl.* **ad·ver·sar·ies.** An opponent, enemy, or foe: *Although the two countries had been adversaries in the past, they worked together on space exploration.*

af·fil·i·ate (ə fĭl′ē āt′) *v.* **af·fil·i·at·ed, af·fil·i·at·ing, af·fil·i·ates.** **1.** To be joined or connected in close association: *Some voters are not affiliated with a political party.* **2.** To associate (oneself) with a larger group: *A local radio station hopes to affiliate with a national network.* **—***n.* A person, group, or organization that is closely joined or connected with a larger or more important body or organization.

af·firm (ə fûrm′) *v.* To declare positively or firmly: *The Supreme Court affirmed that the Bill of Rights guarantees the rights of all citizens.*

af·fix (ə fĭks′) *v.* To fasten; attach: *I almost forgot to affix a stamp to the letter.*

af·flic·tion (ə flĭk′shən) *n.* A state or condition of pain, suffering, or distress: *Beethoven's affliction of deafness did not keep him from composing great symphonies.*

ag·o·nize (ăg′ə nīz′) *v.* **ag·o·nized, ag·o·niz·ing, ag·o·niz·es.** To feel or cause to feel great pain or distress: *I agonized over the decision of what to give my mother for her birthday.*

ag·o·niz·ing (ăg′ə nī′zĭng) *adj.* Causing great pain or distress: *Speaking to a group is an agonizing experience for many people.*

al·ien·ate (āl′yə nāt′ *or* ā′lē ə nāt′) *v.* **al·ien·at·ed, al·ien·at·ing, al·ien·ates.** To cause the loss of friendship or support: *Being rude to friends may alienate them.*

am·bi·dex·trous (ăm′bĭ dĕk′strəs) *adj.* Able to use both hands equally well: *The surgeon was ambidextrous.* **—am′bi·dex′trous·ly** *adv.*

am·biv·a·lent (ăm bĭv′ə lənt) *adj.* Having or showing conflicting feelings about someone, something, or an idea: *The boy is ambivalent about whether he wants to be a doctor or a lawyer.* **—am·biv′a·lent·ly** *adv.*

am·i·ca·ble (ăm′ĭ kə bəl) *adj.* Friendly; peaceable; showing good will: *The two rival teams were amicable toward each other after the game.* **—am′i·ca·bil′i·ty, am′i·ca·ble·ness** *n.* **—am′i·ca·bly** *adv.*

am·o·rous (ăm′ər əs) *adj.* **1.** Relating to, feeling, showing, or expressing love: *Mark wrote an amorous letter to his new wife.* **2.** Attracted to love: *The main character in the movie is an amorous girl.* **—am′or·ous·ly** *adv.*

an·ec·dote (ăn′ĭk dōt′) *n.* A short entertaining account of an interesting incident or event: *My grandfather often entertains us with anecdotes about his childhood.* **—an′ec·dot′al** *adj.*

an·tag·o·nize (ăn tăg′ə nīz′) *v.* **an·tag·o·nized, an·tag·o·niz·ing, an·tag·o·niz·es.** To cause dislike or anger; to make unfriendly: *People should not antagonize their neighbors' dogs by teasing them.*

an·te·bel·lum (ăn′tē bĕl′əm) *adj.* Existing before a war, especially the American Civil War: *Tourists may visit antebellum houses in the South.*

an·te·ce·dent (ăn tĭ sēd′ənt) *n.* **1.** A person, thing, or event that comes before another: *Studying should be an antecedent to a test.* **2.** A noun, phrase, or clause to which a pronoun refers. In the sentence *My dog was hungry, so I fed her,* the noun *dog* is the antecedent of the pronoun *her.*

an·te·date (ăn′tĭ dāt′) *v.* **an·te·dat·ed, an·te·dat·ing, an·te·dates.** **1.** To come before in time; to be of an earlier date: *The invention of the television antedates the invention of the personal computer.* **2.** To put a date on something that is earlier than the actual date: *People should not antedate their checks when paying their bills.*

an·te·room (ăn′tē rōōm′ *or* ăn′tē rŏŏm′) *n.* A waiting room or entrance to a larger room: *The anteroom to the ballroom was filled with guests.*

an·ti·cli·max (ăn′tē klī′măks′) *n.* **1.** Anything that is viewed as a disappointing letdown to what has come before it: *Because it rained, the picnic was an anticlimax to all the preparations for it.* **2.** Something less important or interesting that follows more important or dignified events.

an·ti·dote (ăn′tĭ dōt′) *n.* **1.** A medicine, substance, or remedy that counteracts the effects of poison: *There was an antidote for wasp stings in the first* *aid kit.* **2.** Something that acts as a remedy: *Walking can be an antidote to stress.*

an·tip·a·thy (ăn **tĭp′**ə thē) *n., pl.* **an·tip·a·thies.**
1. A strong feeling of dislike: *The man had an antipathy to flying.* **2.** A person or object that arouses such dislike.

an·ti·sep·tic (ăn′tĭ **sĕp′**tĭk) *adj.* **1.** Free from germs; very clean: *An operating room should be antiseptic.* **2.** Preventing infection or rot by stopping the growth of germs. *—n.* A substance that kills or stops the growth of germs, such as alcohol: *Doctors rub the arm with an antiseptic before giving a shot.*

an·ti·so·cial (ăn′tē **sō′**shəl) *adj.* **1.** Not liking companionship; unwilling to associate with others; unsociable: *The antisocial woman never attended any parties.* **2.** Harmful to the general good of society: *Terrorism is an antisocial act.*

an·ti·tox·in (ăn′tē **tŏk′**sĭn) *n.* **1.** A substance formed in the body that acts against a specific toxin or poison produced by bacteria: *Because his body produced antitoxins against the bacteria, he didn't get ill.* **2.** A serum containing such an antibody obtained from the blood of an animal that has had a particular disease or that has been injected with a toxin.

ap·peal (ə **pēl′**) *n.* **1.** An earnest request or plea, as for help: *The storm was so strong that the captain of the small boat sent an appeal for help.* **2.** A request for someone to decide in one's favor. *—v.* To make a request: *During the flood, the city appealed for people to fill sandbags.*

ap·praise (ə **prāz′**) *v.* **ap·praised, ap·prais·ing, ap·prais·es.** To determine, judge, or estimate the value of: *The buyers wanted their bank to appraise the house.*

ap·pren·tice (ə **prĕn′**tĭs) *n.* **1.** A person who works for another skilled worker in order to learn a trade or craft: *An apprentice learns the work by doing what the boss says to do.* **2.** A student or beginner.

ap·ti·tude (**ăp′**tĭ to̅o̅d′ *or* **ăp′**tĭ tyo̅o̅d′) *n.* **1.** A natural ability, talent, or tendency: *The child showed an aptitude for music.* **2.** Quickness to learn or understand: *The teacher was amazed by the child's aptitude in math.*

as·sets (**ăs′**ĕts′) *n.* All the property and resources owned by a person or business that have a cash value and may be used to pay debts: *Before approving the loan, the bank wanted to know what assets the borrower had.*

a·sun·der (ə **sŭn′**dər) *adv.* **1.** Into separate parts or pieces: *The seaside restaurant was torn asunder by the hurricane.* **2.** Apart from each other: *The papers were blown asunder by the high wind.*

au·to·ma·tion (ô′tə **mā′**shən) *n.* The development and use of machines, electronic devices, computers, or robots that do the work rather than people: *Automation of factories has caused some people to lose their jobs.*

awe (ô) *v.* **awed, aw·ing, awes.** To inspire or fill with wonder, fear, and great respect: *The tourists were awed by the Grand Canyon.* *—n.* A feeling of wonder, fear, great respect: *I am filled with awe when I think of the size of the universe.*

B

ba·bel (**băb′**əl *or* **bā′**bəl) *n.* A confused mixture of many sounds, voices, or languages: *The babel in the crowded room made it impossible for me to have an intelligent conversation.*

badg·er (**băj′**ər) *n.* A mammal with a heavy body, short legs, long claws, and a thick short tail that lives in holes that it has burrowed. It usually feeds at night on insects and smaller animals.—*v.* To continuously annoy, pester, or nag: *The child badgered her mother to buy her a toy.*

ban·ter (**băn′**tər) *n.* Playful, good-natured conversation; joking, or teasing: *The whole class enjoyed the banter between the teacher and the coach.*

ba·sil·i·ca (bə **sĭl′**ĭ kə) *n.* A type of church having two rows of columns on either side and a central hall with two side aisles, ending in a semicircular area: *The wedding was held in a basilica.*

bas·tion (**băs′**chən *or* **băs′**tē ən) *n.* **1.** A part projecting from the main fortification that allows the defenders a wider range of fire. **2.** Anything regarded as firmly protecting some position, place, quality, or condition; stronghold: *Education is the bastion for freedom.*

beast·ly (**bēst′**lē) *adj.* **beast·li·er, beast·li·est. 1.** Like a beast. **2.** Unpleasant; terrible; disagreeable: *The five-mile hike in the cold rain was beastly.*

be·deck (bĭ **dĕk′**) *v.* To cover with decorations or ornaments; adorn: *The wedding cake was bedecked with flowers.*

ber·serk (bər **sûrk′** *or* bər **zûrk′**) *adj. & adv.* In or into a wild, violent, or crazed rage: *A symptom of rabies is berserk behavior.*

be·seech (bĭ **sēch′**) *v.* **be·sought** (bĭ **sôt′**) *or* **be·seeched, be·seech·ing, be·seech·es.** To ask (for) seriously; plead; beg: *The administrator of the shelter for homeless people beseeched the public for donations of food.*

bi·an·nu·al (bī **ăn′**yo̅o̅ əl) *adj.* Happening twice a year; semiannual: *The store has biannual sales in January and July.* **—bi·an′nu·al·ly** *adv.*

bi·cen·ten·ni·al (bī′sĕn **tĕn**′ē əl) *adj.* Happening once every 200 years: *The bicentennial appearance of the comet was a newsworthy event.* —*n.* A 200th anniversary or its celebration: *The city celebrated the bicentennial of its founding.*

bick·er (**bĭk**′ər) *v.* To argue or quarrel over unimportant matters: *The children bickered about where they would sit in the car.*

bi·en·ni·al (bī **ĕn**′ē əl) *adj.* **1.** Happening once every two years: *The biennial elections are held in even years such as 1998 and 2000.* **2.** Lasting for two years: *The flower garden has quite a few biennial plants.* —*n.* A plant that lives for two years, blooming and producing seed in the second year. —**bi·en′ni·al·ly** *adv.*

bi·lat·er·al (bī **lăt**′ər əl) *adj.* **1.** Of, involving, or affecting two sides: *The bilateral treaty was signed by the presidents of both countries.* **2.** Having two sides. —**bi·lat′er·al·ly** *adv.*

bi·lin·gual (bī **lĭng**′gwəl) *adj.* **1.** Able to speak two languages equally well: *The Spanish teacher is bilingual.* **2.** Expressed or written in two languages: *The bilingual book is written in both English and French.*

bi·ome (**bī**′ōm′) *n.* A natural community made up of plants and animals that live in a particular geographical area with a particular climate: *Prairies are a type of biome.*

blas·phe·my (**blăs**′fə mē) *n., pl.* **blas·phe·mies.** A disrespectful remark or act against God or something sacred: *Writing disrespectful words on the walls of a temple is considered blasphemy.*

blight·ed (**blīt**′əd) *adj.* Withered, ruined, or destroyed: *The blighted plants were evidence of the extremely dry summer.*

bo·vine (**bō**′vīn′ *or* **bō**′vēn′) *adj.* **1.** Resembling an ox or cow. **2.** Dull, slow, or stupid: *The teacher gave the class a break when she noticed that the students all had bovine stares on their faces.*

brawn·y (**brô**′nē) *adj.* **brawn·i·er, brawn·i·est.** Muscular and strong; robust: *The brawny weight lifter works out every day.* —**brawn′i·ness** *n.*

breach (brēch) *n.* **1.** A violation of a law, promise, or obligation: *Driving faster than the posted speed limit is a breach of the law.* **2.** A hole, break, or gap made in something solid: *Water came in through the breach in the foundation of the house.*

bul·bous (**bŭl**′bəs) *adj.* **1.** Growing from bulbs: *Daffodils are bulbous plants.* **2.** Shaped like a bulb: *The clown's bulbous nose was not real.*

C

ca·jole (kə **jōl**′) *v.* **ca·joled, ca·jol·ing, ca·joles.** To persuade by flattery, insincere talk, or false promises: *I cajoled my mother into buying me a new violin by promising I would practice an hour every day.*

cam·ou·flage (**kăm**′ə fläzh′ *or* **kăm**′ə fläj′) *n.* **1.** A method used by the military to disguise or conceal troops or equipment to make them blend into the surroundings. **2.** A disguise or appearance that conceals or deceives: *The snake's camouflage made it look like a stick.* —*v.* **cam·ou·flaged, cam·ou·flag·ing, cam·ou·flag·es.** To hide by means of a camouflage: *The troops camouflaged the gun with tree branches and leaves.*

cap·il·lar·y (**kăp**′ə lĕr′ē) *n., pl.* **cap·il·lar·ies.** Any of the tiny blood vessels that connect the arteries with the veins: *The capillary bled for a long time.*

cit·a·del (**sĭt**′ə dəl) *n.* **1.** A fortress or stronghold built to overlook a city: *The citadel was built to protect the city from raiders.* **2.** A stronghold, safe place, or refuge.

clas·sic (**klăs**′ĭk) *adj.* **1.** Serving as a model or outstanding example: *The automobile is a classic example of man's search for faster transportation.* **2.** Typical: *Barking and a wagging tail are classic signs of a dog's excitement.*

cleave (klēv) *v.* **cleft** or **cleaved** or **clove, cleft** or **cleaved** or **cloven, cleaving, cleaves.** To divide or split as by force: *A tornado is able to cleave a building.*

cler·gy (**klûr**′jē) *n., pl.* **cler·gies.** People authorized to conduct religious services, such as ministers, priests, rabbis, or mullahs: *A member of the clergy is authorized to perform weddings.*

co·erce (kō **ûrs**′) *v.* **co·erced, co·erc·ing, co·erc·es.** To persuade or force by threats, pressure, or violence: *The child tried to coerce her sister to play with her by threatening to hide a favorite doll.*

co·he·sive (kō **hē**′sĭ v) *adj.* Capable of or tending to stick or hold together: *Even though our family is large, we are cohesive.* —**co·he′sive·ly** *adv.* —**co·he′sive·ness** *n.*

col·league (**kŏl**′ēg′) *n.* A fellow member of a profession, staff, or organization; coworker; associate: *My colleagues and I like to discuss our projects during lunch.*

come·ly (**kŭm**′lē) *adj.* **come·li·er, come·li·est.** Attractive; fair; good-looking: *Romeo thought that Juliet had a comely appearance.*

com·pel (kəm **pĕl**′) *v.* **com·pelled, compelling, com·pels.** To make people do something necessary by force or demand: *The state compels dri-*

vers to take an eye test when they renew their licenses.

compound interest *n.* Money paid on the original sum of money and the interest previously earned in a savings account: *Since the savings account earned compound interest, the balance grew rapidly.*

com·pre·hen·sive (kŏm′ prĭ **hĕn′**sĭv) *adj.* Covering a great deal; thorough; complete: *The comprehensive investigation led to the solution of the crime.* —**com′ pre·hen′ sive·ly** *adv.*

con·cave (kŏn **kāv′** *or* **kŏn′**kāv′) *adj.* Curved inward like the inside of a circle or bowl: *Children liked to play in the concave structure at the park.* —**con·cave′ ly** *adv.* —**con·cave′ ness** *n.*

con·fute (kən **fyo͞ot′**) *v.* **con·fut·ed, con·fut·ing, con·futes.** To prove to be wrong or false; disprove: *Despite efforts to confute the findings of the study, scientists have not found any evidence that the conclusions are wrong.*

con·geal (kən **jēl′**) *v.* To thicken or change from a liquid to a solid by cooling or freezing: *The gelatin congealed in the refrigerator.*

con·ges·tion (kən **jĕs′**chən) *n.* A condition of overcrowding: *It took a long time to get lunch because of the congestion in the cafeteria.*

con·trived (kən **trīvd′**) *adj.* Obviously or carefully planned: *The author worked for days on the contrived ending of the book.*

con·vex (**kŏn′**vĕks′ *or* kən **vĕks′**) *adj.* Curved outward like the outside of a circle or dome: *The convex shape of the domed stadium was easy to see in the pictures taken from the blimp.* —**con·vex′ ly** *adv.* —**con·vex′ ness** *n.*

co·sign·er (kō **sīn′** ər) *n.* A person who adds his or her signature to (a legal document, such as a contract) and accepts responsibility to fulfill the terms if the other person fails to do so: *His mother was the cosigner for the loan on the house.*

cred·i·tor (**krĕd′** ĭ tər) *n.* A person to whom money is owed: *The creditor sent a bill every month.*

cul·tur·al (**kŭl′**chər əl) *adj.* Of or relating to the way of life, customs, beliefs, and arts of a particular group of people: *It is interesting to learn the cultural differences of people from different countries.* —**cul′ tur·al·ly** *adv.*

D

dank (dăngk) *adj.* **dank·er, dank·est.** Unpleasantly damp; cold and wet: *The inside of the cave was dank.* —**dank ly** *adv.* —**dank ness** *n.*

dap·pled (**dăp′**əld) *adj.* Having spots, streaks, or patches of different colors or shade; spotted: *The grass was dappled with shade from the sun shining through the large trees.*

deb·it (**dĕb′**ĭt) *n.* The money deducted and recorded in an account: *My bank statement showed a debit of $10 for new checks.*

de·crep·it (dĭ **krĕp′**ĭt) *adj.* Broken down, weakened, or worn out because of old age or overuse: *We were afraid that the decrepit car would not make it to our destination.*

de·fault (dĭ **fôlt′**) *v.* **1.** To fail to pay money owed: *After losing his job, Sam had to default on his bank loan.* **2.** To fail to do what is required. —*n.* A failure to do what is required, especially to pay money owed. —**de·fault′ er** *n.*

de·fi·ant (dĭ **fī′**ənt) *adj.* Showing open or bold resistance or contempt to authority or an opponent: *The girl was grounded because of her defiant behavior.* —**de·fi′ ant·ly** *adv.*

de·mise (dĭ **mīz′**) *n.* **1.** Death: *The demise of the famous actor saddened his fans.* **2.** End: *The demise of the company forced many people out of work.*

des·e·cra·tion (dĕs′ ĭ **krā′**shən) *n.* The harming, violation, or destruction of something sacred: *The desecration of the tombstones shocked the townspeople.*

des·ig·na·tion (dĕz′ ĭg **nā′**shən) *n.* **1.** Selection for a particular duty, assignment, or purpose: *The designation of the Valentine's Day king and queen is made by a committee.* **2.** The act of indicating, pointing out, or specifying something: *The designation of the snow-removal route is shown on the city map.*

de·spise (dĭ **spīz′**) *v.* **de·spised, de·spis·ing, de·spis·es.** To hate or show scorn toward: *Even though I despise housework, I know I have to do it.*

de·spon·dent (dĭ **spŏn′**dənt) *adj.* Having lost hope; discouraged; depressed: *The actor was despondent when his movie was unsuccessful at the box offices.* —**de·spon′ dence, de·spon′ den·cy** *n.*

dev·as·tate (**dĕv′**ə stāt′) *v.* **dev·as·tat·ed, dev·as·tat·ing, dev·as·tates.** To lay waste; destroy: *A hurricane can devastate a beach as well as any buildings in its path.* —**dev′ as·tat′ ing·ly** *adv.* —**dev′ as·ta′ tor** *n.*

dif·fer·en·ti·ate (dĭf′ ə **rĕn′**shē āt′) *v.* **dif·fer·en·ti·at·ed, dif·fer·en·ti·at·ing, dif·fer·en·ti·ates.** **1.** To tell the difference between; distinguish between: *Sometimes it is difficult to differentiate between expensive clothes and inexpensive ones.* **2.** To make up the difference: *Hard work can differentiate good grades from bad ones.*

dis·dain (dĭs **dān′**) *v.* To consider or treat as though low or worthless; to scorn: *The rude girl disdained the friendliness of her classmates.* —*n.* A feeling of dislike or scorn for something that is thought to be unworthy or lowly: *The woman's disdain for the simple meal hurt the host's feelings.*

dis·grun·tle (dĭs **grŭn′**tl) *v.* **dis·grun·tled, dis·grun·tling, dis·grun·tles.** To anger: make dissatisfied, disgusted, or displeased: *The poor service disgruntled the customers.* —*adj.* **dis·grun·tled** (dĭs **grŭn′**tld) Dissatisfied; disgusted; angry: *After the fifth loss in a row, the disgruntled football fans booed the team.*

dis·guise (dĭs **gīz′**) *v.* **dis·guised, dis·guis·ing, dis·guis·es.** To hide the real appearance or nature of: *The girl disguised her sadness by smiling.* —*n.* Something that hides.

dis·in·te·grate (dĭs **ĭn′**tĭ grāt′) *v.* **dis·in·te·grat·ed, dis·in·te·grat·ing, dis·in·te·grates.** To separate into small parts; to break up: *When the tide came in, the sand castle disintegrated.*

dis·par·i·ty (dĭ **spăr′**ĭ tē) *n., pl.* **dis·par·i·ties.** Lack of similarity or agreement; inequality; difference: *The mother knew the children were lying because of the disparity in their stories.*

dis·sec·tion (dĭ **sĕk′**shən *or* dī **sĕk′**shən) *n.* **1.** The act of cutting apart for study or scientific examination: *The dissection of the animal was necessary to determine if it had rabies.* **2.** A detailed analysis or examination: *The accountant conducted a dissection of the new tax law.*

dog·ged (**dô′**gĭd *or* **dŏg′**ĭd) *adj.* Not giving up; persistent; stubborn: *The girl's dogged determination to be a doctor paid off when she got her degree.* —**dog′ged·ly** *adv.* —**dog′ged·ness** *n.*

dom·i·nate (**dŏm′**ə nāt′) *v.* **dom·i·nat·ed, dom·i·nat·ing, dom·i·nates.** To have the main influence or control; to rule over: *Talk shows dominate daytime television.*

drab (drăb) *adj.* **drab·ber, drab·best.** Lacking brightness; dull; dreary; faded: *The drab carpet did not match the bright walls.* —*n.* A dull, grayish or yellowish brown. —**drab′ly** *adv.* —**drab′ness** *n.*

drudg·er·y (**drŭj′**ə rē) *n., pl.* **drudg·er·ies.** Boring, tiresome, or unpleasant work: *Weeding the garden in the hot sun may seem like drudgery.*

E

e·go·tis·ti·cal (ē′gə **tĭs′**tĭ kəl) *adj.* Conceited; self-centered: *I get tired of hearing egotistical people boast about themselves.* —**e′go·tis′ti·cal·ly** *adv.*

e·lim·i·nate (ĭ **lĭm′**ə nāt′) *v.* **e·lim·i·nat·ed, e·lim·i·nat·ing, e·lim·i·nates. 1.** To get rid of; remove: *It is difficult to eliminate all bad habits.* **2.** To leave out of consideration: *After the first race all but the two fastest runners were eliminated.*

el·lip·ti·cal (ĭ **lĭp′**tĭ kəl) *adj.* Of, relating to, or shaped like an oval with both ends alike: *Although the elliptical window was unusual, it was beautiful.* —**el·lip′ti·cal·ly** *adv.*

em·i·nent (**ĕm′**ə nənt) *adj.* Above all others, as in power, rank, position; famous; distinguished: *The eminent writer was gracious when she accepted the award for her latest book.* —**em′i·nent·ly** *adv.*

e·mis·sion (ĭ **mĭsh′**ən) *n.* **1.** Something that is released, discharged, or sent out: *Many states require that car exhaust systems be tested for dangerous emissions.* **2.** The act or process of releasing, discharging, or sending out.

en·chant (ĕn **chănt′**) *v.* **1.** To place under a spell; bewitch: *Merlin was able to enchant people.* **2.** To charm: *The music enchanted the audience.* **3.** To be under a spell or bewitched: *Hansel and Gretel were enchanted by the witch.*

en·com·pass (ĕn **kŭm′**pəs) *v.* **en·com·passed, en·com·pass·ing, en·com·pass·es. 1.** To include; contain: *Although the historical novel is fiction, it encompasses real events from the l800s.* **2.** To surround; encircle: *A fence encompasses the ranch.*

en·cum·brance (ĕn **kŭm′**brəns) *n.* A person or thing that stands in the way; something that burdens or hinders: *Not knowing how to type was an encumbrance to getting the job.*

en·hance (ĕn **hăns′**) *v.* **en·hanced, en·hanc·ing, en·hanc·es.** To make greater or better, as in value, reputation, or quality: *The actress's beauty was enhanced by her makeup.* —**en·hance′ment** *n.*

en·sure (ĕn **shoŏr′**) *v.* **en·sured, en·sur·ing, en·sures.** To make sure; guarantee: *Consistently doing one's homework helps to ensure good grades in school.*

e·rad·i·cate (ĭ **răd′**ĭ kāt′) *v.* **e·rad·i·cat·ed, e·rad·i·cat·ing, e·rad·i·cates.** To get rid of; remove; destroy completely: *Scientists hope to eradicate many diseases through the use of vaccinations.* **e·rad′i·ca′tion** *n.*

e·ro·sion (ĭ **rō′**zhən) *n.* The gradual wearing, washing, or eating away, especially of rock or soil, by wind, water, or glaciers: *The erosion of fertile soil is a problem for farmers.*

e·soph·a·gus (ĭ **sŏf′**ə gəs) *n., pl.* **e·soph·a·gi.** The tube or passageway connecting the throat and the stomach: *Food passes from the throat through the esophagus to the stomach.*

es·trange (ĭ strānj′) *v.* **es·tranged, es·trang·ing, es·trang·es.** To cause (someone) to change from friendly or kind feelings to unfriendly or unkind feelings: *I do not want to estrange my friends by telling lies about them.* —**es·trange′ment** *n.*

et·i·quette (ĕt′ĭ kĕt′ *or* ĕt′ĭ kĭt) *n.* The rules and forms of proper behavior required in society or business: *People often take classes in etiquette so that they will know how to act in formal situations.*

e·volve (ĭ vŏlv′) *v.* **e·volved, e·volv·ing, e·volves.**
1. To develop gradually: *The idea for the book evolved over several years.* **2.** *Biology.* To undergo the development or change of organisms or species from their original state to their present state.

ex·ac·er·bate (ĭg zăs′ər bāt′) *v.* **ex·ac·er·bat·ed, ex·ac·er·bat·ing, ex·ac·er·bates.** To make worse, more intense or severe; aggravate: *The second ice storm in a week exacerbated the icy condition of the roads.*

ex·ca·vate (ĕk′skə vāt′) *v.* **ex·ca·vat·ed, ex·ca·vat·ing, ex·ca·vates. 1.** To uncover by digging: *Archaeologists excavated the ancient city of Pompeii.* **2.** To make a hole in; hollow out: *The workers excavated under the English Channel to build the Chunnel.* **3.** To remove by digging: *A shovel was used to excavate the dirt.*

ex·cel (ĭk sĕl′) *v.* **ex·celled, ex·cel·ling, ex·cels.** To be better or greater than, as in ability; outdo; surpass: *The Hall of Fame baseball player excels in pitching.*

ex·e·cute (ĕk′sĭ kyo͞ot′) *v.* **ex·e·cut·ed, ex·e·cut·ing, ex·e·cutes. 1.** To carry out; to put into effect: *Schools execute the law that students must have up-to-date immunizations to attend classes.* **2.** To do; perform: *The ice skater executed a very complicated jump.* **3.** To create or produce something, such as a work of art, according to a plan or design: *The sculptor executed a lifelike statue.*

ex·pan·sion (ĭk spăn′shən) *n.* The act of growing in size, number, volume, or scope: *The expansion of the use of computers will continue into the next century.*

ex·pa·tri·ate (ĕk spā′trē āt′) *v.* **ex·pa·tri·at·ed, ex·pa·tri·at·ing, ex·pa·tri·ates. 1.** To remove someone from his or her native country. **2.** To voluntarily remove oneself from living in one's native country. —*n.* (ek spa′trē ĭt) A person who voluntarily lives in a foreign country: *During the French Revolution many French noblemen became expatriates in other European countries.* —**ex·pa′tri·a′tion** *n.*

ex·pe·di·ent (ĭk spē′dē ənt) *n.* A way to achieve the desired result: *Calling 911 is a quick expedient for getting emergency help.* —*adj.* Suitable or convenient for a particular purpose: *Using the microwave oven is an expedient way to prepare a meal quickly.*

ex·pel (ĭk spĕl′) *v.* **ex·pelled, ex·pel·ling, ex·pels. 1.** To force to leave: *A student may be expelled for bringing a weapon to school.* **2.** To force out, drive out, eject: *Take a deep breath and expel the air slowly.*

ex·ten·sive (ĭk stĕn′sĭv) *adj.* Widespread; large in amount; vast; far-reaching: *Extensive research is done to determine if a new medicine is safe for people to use.*

ex·ter·mi·nate (ĭk stûr′mə nāt′) *v.* **ex·ter·mi·nat·ed, ex·ter·mi·nat·ing, ex·ter·mi·nates.** To destroy completely; to wipe out: *We had to exterminate the termites before we could move into the house.* —**ex·ter′mi·na′tion** *n.*

ex·tinct (ĭk stĭngkt′) *adj.* No longer living or in existence: *There are many theories about why dinosaurs became extinct.*

ex·trem·i·ty (ĭk strĕm′ĭ tē) *n., pl.* **ex·trem·i·ties. 1.** The farthest or outermost part: *The tip of Cape Cod is the extremity of Massachusetts.* **2.** The hands and feet: *The extremities need protection from frostbite.*

ex·u·ber·ant (ĭg zo͞o′bər ənt) *adj.* Overflowing with joy, high spirits, or unrestrained enthusiasm: *The fans were exuberant when their team won the state championship.* —**ex·u′ber·ant·ly** *adv.*

F

fer·ret (fĕr′ĭt) *v.* To find out by searching; uncover: *The baseball card collector ferreted out old cards at garage sales.* —*n.* An animal from the polecat family that is sometimes trained to hunt rats, mice, and rabbits.

fer·vid (fûr′vĭd) *adj.* Having or showing great emotion or warmth of feeling; enthusiastic: *The Olympic swimmer had a fervid desire to win a gold medal.* —**fer′vid·ly** *adv.* —**fer′vid·ness** *n.*

fick·le (fĭk′əl) *adj.* Changeable, especially with one's affections for others: *The fickle boy had a different girlfriend every day.* —**fick′le·ness** *n.*

flex·i·ble (flĕk′sə bəl) *adj.* **1.** Capable of adjusting to change: *A teacher must be flexible since students have different learning styles.* **2.** Able to be bent: *The hose is flexible.* —**flex′i·bil′i·ty** *n.* —**flex′i·bly** *adv.*

for·age (fôr′ĭj *or* fŏr′ĭj) *v.* **for·aged, for·ag·ing, for·ag·es. 1,** To search or hunt for food: *The raccoon foraged in the forest.* **2.** To search for something. *n.* **1.** Food for horses or cattle. **2.** The search for food. —**for′ag·er** *n.*

fore·close (fôr **klōz′**) *v.* **fore·closed, fore·clos·ing, fore·clos·es.** To take away the right to pay off (a mortgage) usually by taking the property, especially after failure to make payments on the loan: *The bank foreclosed on the house because no mortgage payments had been made for six months.*

for·mi·da·ble (fôr′mǐ də bəl) *adj.* **1.** Difficult to defeat, deal with, or do: *Climbing Mt. Everest is a formidable challenge.* **2.** Causing fear, dread, or awe. **—for′mi·da·bil′i·ty** *n.* **—for′mi·da·bly** *adv.*

fu·ry (fyoor′ē) *n., pl.* **fu·ries. 1.** Violent anger; rage: *The man's fury frightened everyone in the room.* **2.** Violence; fierceness: *Beware of a mother bear's fury when she is protecting her cubs.*

G

gar·ner (gär′nər) *v.* **1.** To earn or collect: *The new symphony conductor garnered praise from the music critics.* **2.** To gather and store: *Squirrels garner acorns for the winter.*

gen·er·a·tion (jěn′ə rā′shən) *n.* **1.** A group of people born and living about the same time: *The younger generation often likes different music than older generations enjoy.* **2.** One step in the line of natural descent: *There were three generations at the family reunion—grandparents, parents, and children.*

ge·net·ic (jə nět′ĭk) *adj.* Of or relating to inherited characteristics found in similar or related organisms: *Sisters have the same genetic makeup.* **—ge·net′i·cal·ly** *adv.*

gen·ial (jēn′yəl) *adj.* **1.** Pleasant; cheerful; friendly: *The genial neighbors invited everyone on the block to a barbecue.* **2.** Good for life and growth; comfortably warm and mild. *People like to live in a genial climate.* **—ge′ni·al′i·ty** *n.* **gen′ial·ly** *adv.*

gen·try (jěn′trē) *n., pl.* **gen·tries.** People of high social standing and good family: *Most of the local gentry belong to an exclusive club.*

ge·o·met·ric (jē′ə mět′rĭk) *adj.* **1.** Of or relating to the characteristics, measurements, and relationships of lines, surfaces, and figures. **2.** Made of or using straight lines, angles, or circles: *The geometric design drawn on the computer was very interesting.* **—ge′o·met′ri·cal·ly** *adv.*

ger·mi·nate (jûr′mə nāt′) *v.* **ger·mi·nat·ed, ger·mi·nat·ing, ger·mi·nates.** To start or cause to start to grow or develop; sprout: *The flower seeds began to germinate a week after they were planted.* **—ger′mi·na′tion** *n.* **—ger′mi·na·tor′** *n.*

H

hu·man (hyoo′mən) *adj.* Having the qualities of a living person: *Scientists are constantly studying the human body.* **—n.** A person.

hu·mane (hyoo mān′) *adj.* Having or showing kindness, mercy, compassion, or sympathy: *The animal shelter was known for its humane treatment of lost pets.* **—hu·mane′ly** *adv.*

hy·per·ac·tive (hī′pər ăk′tĭv) *adj.* Highly or overly active: *The hyperactive child had difficulty sitting still for even a few minutes.*

hy·per·bo·le (hī pûr′bə lē) *n.* An intentional exaggeration that is not meant to be taken literally: *Everyone laughed at the hyperbole about how hot it was outside.*

hy·per·ex·ten·sion (hī′pər ĭk stěn′shən) *n.* The act of straightening or extending a bodily joint beyond its normal range of motion: *A hyperextension of the knee is very painful.*

hy·per·son·ic (hī′pər sŏn′ĭk) *adj.* Moving at a rate of at least five times the speed of sound: *We heard the sound of the hypersonic jet quite a few seconds after we saw it.*

hy·per·ten·sion (hī′pər těn′shən) *n.* High blood pressure: *People with hypertension should see their doctors regularly.*

hy·po·chon·dri·ac (hī′pə kŏn′drē ăk′) *n.* A person who worries excessively that he or she is ill or is becoming ill: *The hypochondriac talked only about his poor health.*

hy·poc·ri·sy (hī pŏk′rĭ sē) *n., pl.* **hy·poc·ri·sies.** The practice of showing or stating feelings, beliefs, or qualities that one does not possess: *The hypocrisy of the candidate became evident after she was elected.*

hy·po·der·mic (hī pə dûr′mĭk) *adj.* **1.** Beneath the skin. **2.** Injected or used to inject under the skin: *The shot was given with a long hypodermic needle.* **—n.** An injection given under the skin with a needle.

hy·pot·e·nuse (hī pŏt′n oos′ *or* hī pŏt′n yoos′) *n.* The side of a right triangle opposite the right angle: *The teacher told the students to find the hypotenuse of the triangle.*

hy·po·thet·i·cal (hī′pə thět′ĭ kəl) *adj.* Based on a theory; theoretical: *The hypothetical explanation sounded logical even though it had not been proven.* **—hy′po·thet′i·cal·ly** *adv.*

I

ig·ni·tion (ĭg nĭsh′ən) *n.* The act or process of setting on fire, burning, or catching on fire: *The ignition of the gasoline caused a terrible fire.*

im·merse (ĭ **mûrs'**) v. **im·mersed, im·mers·ing, im·mers·es. 1.** To completely cover with water or other liquid; submerge: *When it is very hot, it is refreshing to immerse oneself in a swimming pool.* **2.** To involve deeply; absorb: *A wonderful way to spend a rainy afternoon is to immerse oneself in a good book.*

im·mor·tal (ĭ **môr'**tl) adj. **1.** Living forever; never dying: *Human beings are not immortal.* **2.** Remembered or having eternal fame: *The words of the Declaration of Independence are immortal.*

im·pair (ĭm **pâr'**) v. To weaken or make worse the quality, strength, or quantity of; damage: *After I was hit in the eye by a ball, my eyesight was impaired.* **—im·pair'ment** n.

im·pas·sive (ĭm **păs'**ĭv) adj. Not showing or feeling emotion: *The accused burglar was impassive as the verdict was read.* **—im·pas'sive·ly** adv. **—im·pas'sive·ness** n.

im·plore (ĭm **plôr'**) v. **im·plored, im·plor·ing, im·plores. 1.** To plead with; earnestly ask: *The child implored her mother for the new toy.* **2.** To plead, beg, or ask earnestly for: *He implored understanding from his friend.*

im·promp·tu (ĭm **prŏmp'**tōō or ĭm **prŏmp'**tyōō) adj. Spoken, made, or done without previous preparation; offhand: *I planned to be only a spectator at the dedication, but instead I gave an impromptu speech.*

im·pulse (**ĭm'**pŭls') n. **1.** A sudden urge or force that makes a person act without thinking: *I was so happy that I had an impulse to laugh out loud.* **2.** A driving force that causes motion.

in·ar·tic·u·late (ĭn'är **tĭk'**yə lĭt) adj. **1.** Not clearly pronounced or spoken: *The inarticulate speech was impossible to understand.* **2.** Unable to express oneself clearly or meaningfully: *The contestant was so nervous that she was inarticulate.* **—in'ar·tic'u·late·ly** adv. **in'ar·tic'u·late·ness** n.

in·car·cer·a·tion (ĭn kär'sər **ā'**shən) n. Imprisonment: *The incarceration of the convicted criminal lasted for ten years.*

in·clem·ent (ĭn **klĕm'**ənt) adj. Stormy; rough; severe: *The inclement weather forced the closing of many schools.* **—in·clem'en·cy** n.

in·con·spic·u·ous (ĭn'kən **spĭk'**yōō əs) adj. Attracting little attention; not noticeable; not easily seen: *The shy boy wanted to be inconspicuous in the crowded room.*

in·dig·nant (ĭn **dĭg'**nənt) adj. Angry because of something unfair, cruel, evil, or unworthy: *Many people were indignant about the abuse of the dog.* **—in·dig'nant·ly** adv.

in·dis·creet (ĭn dĭ **skrēt'**) adj. Not showing good judgment or tact; unwise: *Leon lost his job because he made indiscreet statements.* **—in'dis·creet'ly** adv. **—in'dis·creet'ness** n.

in·duc·tion (ĭn **dŭk'**shən) n. The process or ceremony of being formally installed in office or brought into a group: *The induction of class officers is held at the beginning of the school year.*

in·flu·en·tial (ĭn'flōō **ĕn'**shəl) adj. Having or exercising the power to produce an effect on or change an event: *Many people think that television programs have become too influential in the lives of young people.* **—in'flu·en'tial·ly** adv.

in·sig·nif·i·cant (ĭn sĭg **nĭf'**ĭ kənt) adj. **1.** Of little or no importance or meaning: *The babbling of the baby was insignificant.* **2.** Small in size, amount, or value: *The number of people at the meeting was insignificant.* **—in'sig·nif'i·cance** n. **—in'sig·nif'i·cant·ly** adv.

in·tent·ly (ĭn **tĕnt'**lē) adv. With close attention: *The baby intently watched his mother's every move.*

in·var·i·a·bly (ĭn **vâr'**ē ə blē) adv. Goes on constantly without change: *The teacher invariably will call on me when I don't know the answer to the question.*

in·ver·sion (ĭn **vûr'**zhən or ĭn **vûr'**shən) n. **1.** The act of turning upside down or the state of being turned upside down: *The inversion of the hummingbird feeder allowed the liquid to slowly drip into the bowl.* **2.** Something that is turned upside down.

in·vul·ner·a·ble (ĭn **vŭl'**nər ə bəl) adj. Impossible to harm, injure, or attack: *The castle was invulnerable because of the moat around it.* **—in·vul'ner·a·bil'i·ty** n.

ir·ra·tion·al (ĭ **răsh'**ə nəl) adj. **1.** Not able to reason or think clearly: *The survivors of the plane crash were irrational for several hours.* **2.** Not based on reason; senseless; absurd: *The child had an irrational fear of the dark.* **—ir·ra'tion·al·ly** adv.

ir·re·deem·a·ble (ĭr'ĭ **dē'**mə bəl) adj. **1.** Not able to be changed or reformed; hopeless: *The irredeemable shopper went to the malls every Saturday.* **2.** That cannot be brought back or paid off: *The expired coupon is irredeemable.*

ir·ref·u·ta·ble (ĭ **rĕf'**yə tə bəl or ĭr ĭ **fyōō'**tə bəl) adj. Impossible to prove wrong or false: *The astronomer claimed that the discovery of the comet was irrefutable.* **—ir·ref'u·ta·bly** adv.

ir·rel·e·vant (ĭ **rĕl'**ə vənt) adj. Not having any connection with the matter at hand; beside the point: *The question about the movie was irrelevant to our discussion of sports.* **—ir·rel'e·vance** n. **—ir·rel'e·vant·ly** adv.

ir·re·triev·a·ble (ĭr ĭ **trē′**və bəl) *adj.* Difficult or impossible to get back or recover: *The family pictures were irretrievable after the fire.*

J

jour·ney·man (**jûr′**nē mən) *n.* A person who has completed training, is skilled in a trade or craft, and works for another person: *It was obvious that the carpenter was a journeyman because his work was excellent.*

jo·vi·al (**jō′**vē əl) *adj.* Full of fun and playful good humor; jolly: *The jovial speaker soon had her audience laughing.* **—jo′vi·al′i·ty** *n.* **jo′vi·al·ly** *adv.*

K

Ko·ran (kə **răn′** *or* kə **rän′**) *n.* The sacred book of Islam, containing the religious and moral code: *The Muslims study the Koran.*

ko·sher (**kō′**shər) *adj.* Conforming to or prepared according to Jewish dietary laws: *The woman bought kosher meat at the market.*

L

la·bo·ri·ous (lə **bôr′**ē əs) *adj.* Difficult and demanding; requiring hard work: *Building the scenery for the play was laborious work.* **la·bo′ri·ous·ly** *adv.* **—la·bo′ri·ous·ness** *n.*

lack·ey (**lăk′**ē) *n., pl.* **lack·eys.** A person who takes or follows orders in the manner of a servant: *The woman wanted a job where she could make decisions and not just be a lackey.*

lack·lus·ter (**lăk′**lŭs′tər) *adj.* Lacking brightness, brilliance, or interest; dull; boring: *The new movie did poorly at the box-office because of the actors' lackluster performance.*

lag·gard (**lăg′**ərd) *n.* A person who falls behind and does not keep up: *The track team lost the meet because the laggard lost his race.* **—adj.** Falling behind; slow: *The laggard hiker got lost.*

la·i·ty (**lā′**ĭ tē) *n.* Members of a religious group that are not the officials: *The laity of the church met to choose a new pastor.*

lame duck (**lām** dŭk) *n.* **1.** An elected official who has not been reelected but continues to hold office until the successor takes over: *Because he was a lame duck, the governor did not introduce any new legislation.* **2.** A weak or useless person: *After I announced my retirement I felt like a lame duck.*

lam·poon (lăm **poon′**) *n.* A piece of writing that uses humor, irony, or exaggeration to make fun of or attack someone or something: *Even though the lampoon of the city council meeting was funny, it upset some people.* **—v.** To make fun of with a lampoon.

lar·ce·nous (**lär′**sə nəs) *adj.* Of, relating to, or involving the theft of another person's property: *The criminal was sentenced to five years in prison for larcenous crimes.*

lar·ynx (**lăr′**ĭngks) *n., pl.* **la·ryn·ges** (lə **rin′**jez) *or* **lar·ynx·es.** The structure at the upper end of the windpipe, containing the vocal cords: *Because of an injury to my larynx, I couldn't talk.*

las·civ·i·ous (lə **sĭv′**ē əs) *adj.* Feeling or showing strong sexual desire; containing sexual material; obscene; indecent: *The lascivious movie was rated R.* **—las·civ′i·ous·ly** *adv.*

lech·er·ous (**lĕch′**ər əs) *adj.* Given to, characterized by, or showing excessive sexual desire or activity; lewd: *The woman sued the man for his lecherous behavior.*

le·sion (**lē′**zhən) *n.* A wound, injury, or abnormal change of an organ or tissue: *The lesion on the toddler's head was caused when he fell and hit his head on the sidewalk.*

le·thal (**lē′**thəl) *adj.* Causing or capable of causing death; deadly: *A lethal injection of poison was the cause of death.*

li·a·bil·i·ty (lī′ ə **bĭl′**ĭ tē) *n., pl.* **li·a·bil·i·ties.** Something for which one is legally responsible, especially an obligation to pay a debt: *When planning a budget, one needs to know what liabilities one has.*

lib·er·a·tion (lĭb′ə **rā′**shən) *n.* The act of setting free or the state of being set free: *The liberation of the prisoners from the Bastille in Paris, France, marked the beginning of the French Revolution.*

lien (lēn *or* **lē′**ən) *n.* A legal claim on another's property for payment of a debt: *The remodeling company placed a lien on the house because the homeowner refused to pay the bill.*

lig·a·ment (**lĭg′**ə mənt) *n.* A band of strong tissue that connects two bones or holds organs in place: *The athlete needed knee surgery to repair the torn ligaments.*

Lil·li·pu·tian (lĭl′ə **pyōō′**shən) *adj.* Tiny: *The Lilliputian dolls were so small that they fit in the palm of the baby's hand.*

lim·er·ick (**lĭm′**ər ĭk) *n.* A humorous five-line poem with the rhyme scheme of *aabba*: *The limericks were such funny poems that we couldn't stop laughing.*

lin·e·ar (**lĭn′**ē ər) *adj.* **1.** Of, relating to, made, or using a line or lines: *The linear drawing of the house was done in ink.* **2.** Relating to length: *The linear measurement of the room is fifteen feet.*

li·on·ize (lī′ə nīz′) *v.* **li·on·ized, li·on·iz·ing, li·on·iz·es.** To treat as a very important person: *People lionize Olympic athletes.*

loath·some (lō*th*′ səm *or* lō*th*′ səm) *adj.* Extremely hateful or disgusting; detestable: *Being cruel to pets is loathsome.*

lux·u·ri·ant (lŭg zhŏŏr′ē ənt *or* lŭk shŏŏr′ē ənt) *adj.* Growing vigorously and abundantly: *The luxuriant flower garden has dozens of healthy plants.*

M

mam·moth (măm′əth) *n.* A very large extinct prehistoric elephant that had long tusks and thick shaggy hair. —*adj.* Huge; giganic: *It took a month to complete the mammoth research project.*

ma·ni·a·cal (mə nī′ə kəl) *adj.* Mentally ill; insane; mad: *The maniacal behavior was the result of a reaction to a drug.*

man·u·script (măn′yə skrĭpt′) *n.* **1.** A book or document written or copied by hand: *The original manuscript of the Declaration of Independence is carefully preserved.* **2.** The handwritten, typewritten, computer-produced version of a book or article that is submitted for publication.

mar·i·tal (măr′ĭ tl) *adj.* Relating to marriage: *The husband and wife attended a class on marital happiness.*

mar·row (măr′ō) *n.* The soft, fatty tissue that fills the cavities inside most bones and that produces blood cells: *The doctor recommended a bone marrow transplant in order to cure the disease.*

mar·tial (mär′shəl) *adj.* **1.** Related to war, the armed forces, or the military life: *The cadet took martial training for six months.* **2.** Warlike; like a warrior.

mec·ca (mĕk′ə) *n.* A place that is the center of important activity or interest: *The space center is a mecca for those who want to be astronauts.*

med·dle (mĕd′l) *v.* **med·dled, med·dling, med·dles.** To interfere in the business or affairs of other people: *A good friend will not meddle in her friend's business.*

med·dle·some (mĕd′l səm) *adj.* Tending to interfere in the business or affairs of other people: *The girl told her meddlesome friend to mind her own business.*

me·dic·i·nal (mĭ dĭs′ə nəl) *adj.* Having the ability to act like a medicine: *Native Americans knew the medicinal qualities of many plants.*

mel·an·chol·y (mĕl′ən kŏl′e) *adj.* **1.** Sad; depressed; gloomy: *The people were melancholy as they left the funeral.* **2.** Causing sadness: *The melancholy poem made the reader cry.* —*n.* Sadness; depression.

me·ni·al (mē′nē əl *or* mēn′yəl) *adj.* Lowly; degrading: *The teenager did menial jobs like sweeping the floors and emptying the trash.*

me·no·rah (mə nôr′ə) *n.* A candleholder, traditionally with seven or nine branches, used in Jewish religious ceremonies: *The lighting of the menorah is an important part of the Hanukkah celebration.*

me·tab·o·lism (mĭ tăb′ə lĭz′əm) *n.* The chemical and physical processes by which a living thing maintains life. Metabolism is the body's process by which food is changed into the energy necessary to carry on all basic life processes.

me·tal·lic (mə tăl′ĭk) *adj.* Of, relating to, or having the qualities of metals, such as lead, copper, iron, and similar elements: *The fall leaves sometimes have a metallic gleam.*

met·tle (mĕt′l) *n.* **1.** Courage; daring; spirit: *The mettle of the movie's hero was an inspiration to all the characters.* **2.** The basic character or quality of a person: *A test of a person's mettle is how he or she deals with problems.*

mold (mōld) *v.* To work into a particular shape or form: *The sculptor began to mold the clay into a vase.* —*n.* **1.** A hollow form used for shaping something. **2.** Something made in a mold.

mor·al (môr′əl *or* mŏr′əl) *n.* A lesson or principle taught by a fable, event, or story: *The moral of the story is that winning takes hard work.* —*adj.* Relating to a standard of right and wrong: *The class discussed whether or not the actions of the story's main character were moral.*

mo·rale (mə răl′) *n.* The state of a person's or group's spirit, attitude, or mental state with respect to qualities like cheerfulness, courage, or confidence: *After winning three games in a row, the team's morale was very high.*

mor·tal·i·ty (môr tăl′ĭ tē) *n., pl.* **mor·tal·i·ties.** The condition or state of being subject to death: *Daredevils seem not to worry about their mortality.*

mor·ti·cian (môr tĭsh′ən) *n.* Someone who arranges funerals and prepares dead people for burial; funeral director; undertaker: *The mortician arranged the funeral for my grandmother.*

mosque (mŏsk) *n.* A Muslim place, house, or temple of worship: *The mosque was filled with worshipers.*

mul·lah (mŭl′ə *or* mŏŏl′ə) *n.* A male religious teacher or leader: *The mullah interpreted the religious law for the people.*

mun·dane (mŭn dān′ *or* mŭn′dān′) *adj.* Common; ordinary: *Sometimes doing mundane tasks like weeding the garden will help relieve stress.*

mu·ta·tion (myo͞o tā′shən) *n.* **1.** A change in genes or chromosomes of living things that can be inherited by their offspring: *The mutation of the gene was responsible for the disease.* **2.** A change: *Mutation of languages happens slowly.*

N

nar·cis·sism (när′sĭ sĭz′əm) *n.* Too much love or admiration for oneself; self-love: *The boy's narcissism was annoying because he constantly bragged about himself.*

nep·o·tism (nĕp′ə tĭz′əm) *n.* The giving of favors or jobs to relatives by someone in an official or high office: *When the senator gave his son a job, he was accused of nepotism.*

neu·tral·ize (no͞o′trə līz′ *or* nyo͞o′trə līz′) *v.* **neu·tral·ized, neu·tral·iz·ing, neu·tral·iz·es.** To make powerless or counteract the effect or force of: *The medicine was able to neutralize the effects of the wasp sting.*

O

of·fen·sive (ə fĕn′sĭv) *adj.* **1.** Causing resentment, anger, or displeasure; insulting: *The offensive remark was inexcusable.* **2.** Unpleasant or disagreeable to the senses: *The smell of the rotten eggs was offensive.* —**of·fen′sive·ly** *adv.*

o·rig·i·nate (ə rĭj′ə nāt′) *v.* **o·rig·i·nat·ed, o·rig·i·nat·ing, o·rig·i·nates.** To start, bring, or come into being: *Many everyday products were originated for the space program.*

or·tho·pe·dic (ôr′thə pē′dĭk) *adj.* Of, relating, or used in the branch of medicine that corrects or treats disorders, diseases, or injuries of the bones, tendons, ligaments, muscles, and joints: *An orthopedic doctor often treats athletes who injure their bones, ligaments, or muscles.*

P

pal·lid (păl′ĭd) *adj.* Lacking color; pale: *The roller coaster ride was so frightening that many riders were pallid when they got off of it.*

pan·de·mo·ni·um (păn′də mō′nē əm) *n.* Wild disorder, confusion, and noise; uproar: *After the football team won the championship, there was pandemonium in the stadium.*

par·a·sit·ic (păr′ə sĭt′ĭk) *adj.* Of or like a parasite, which is an animal or plant that lives on or in another animal or plant from which it gets its food: *A parasitic person takes advantage of another person for his or her own good.*

peal (pēl) *n.* **1.** A loud ringing of bells: *The peal of the church bells announced that the wedding was about to begin.* **2.** A loud burst of sound or noise: *A peal of laughter followed the comedian's joke.*

per·il·ous (pĕr′ə ləs) *adj.* Dangerous; hazardous: *The canoe trip over the steep falls was perilous.*

per·son·i·fied (pər sŏn′ə fīd′) *v.* Past tense of **personify.**

per·son·i·fy (pər sŏn′ə fī′) *v.* **per·son·i·fied, per·son·i·fy·ing, per·son·i·fies.** **1.** To typify or be the perfect example of something, such as a quality or idea. *The child's laughter personified everyone's enjoyment of the fair.* **2.** To give human qualities to an idea or thing: *Some people personify their plants by talking to them.*

per·vade (pər vād′) *v.* **per·vad·ed, per·vad·ing, per·vades.** To spread or be present throughout: *The odor from the barbecue pervaded the park.*

phy·sique (fĭ zēk′) *n.* The form, development, and appearance of the body: *Hercules had a muscular physique.*

pit·fall (pĭt′fôl′) *n., pl.* **pit·falls. 1.** Hidden or unsuspected danger or difficulty: *Without careful planning, a traveler can run into many pitfalls.* **2.** A hidden hole dug into to the ground to trap animals.

pol·y·gon (pŏl′ē gŏn′) *n.* A closed geometric figure having three or more straight lines: *A rectangle is a polygon, but not all polygons are rectangles.*

post·mor·tem (pōst môr′təm) *n.* A medical examination of a dead body to find out the cause of death; autopsy: *After the man died suddenly, a postmortem was done.* —*adj.* Happening or done after death: *The postmortem examination revealed he died of a heart attack.*

po·ten·tial (pə tĕn′shəl) *n.* Possibility: *The potential for thunderstorms was increased by very hot humid weather.* —*adj.* Capable of being but not yet actual: *The talented actor is a potential star.*

pre·pon·der·ance (prĭ pŏn′dər əns) *n.* Superiority in number, weight, force, importance, influence, or power: *The preponderance of evidence showed that the accused person was guilty.*

pri·mar·i·ly (prī mâr′ə lē *or* prī mĕr′ə lē) *adv.* Mainly; chiefly; principally: *The radio station primarily plays classical music.*

probe (prōb) *v.* **probed, prob·ing, probes.** To investigate, explore, or examine thoroughly: *The aviation experts probed the cause of the airline crash.* —*n.* **1.** A thorough investigation: *The probe of the crime ended in an arrest.* **2.** A device, exploratory action, or expedition used for exploration or investigation: *The space probe on Mars was a huge success.*

pro·lif·er·a·tion (prə lĭf′ ə **rā′** shən) *n.* A rapid increase in number or growth: *In the past few years there has been a proliferation of people interested in the Internet.*

prom·i·nent (**prŏm′** ə nənt) *adj.* **1.** Very noticeable; conspicuous: *The Arch is a prominent feature of the St. Louis riverfront.* **2.** Well-known; distinguished: *The Chief Justice is a prominent member of the Supreme Court.* **prom′i·nent·ly** *adv.*

prompt (prŏmpt) *v.* To encourage, urge, or inspire to action: *My success in the local contest prompted me to enter the state contest.* —*adj.* Being on time: *I am always prompt for an appointment.* — **prompt′ ly** *adv.* —**prompt′ ness** *n.*

pro·pel (prə **pĕl′**) *v.* **pro·pelled, pro·pel·ling, pro·pels.** To cause to move forward or to keep in motion: *Wind in the sails propels a sailboat.*

pro·por·tion (prə **pôr′** shən) *n.* **1.** The relationship in size, amount, or degree of one thing to another: *The proportion of girls to boys in the class is the same.* **2. proportions.** Size; dimensions: *The number of hungry people in the world is of huge proportions.*

pro·pul·sion (prə **pŭl′** shən) *n.* **1.** A force that drives forward: *A strong push was the propulsion that the go-cart needed.* **2.** The act of driving forward.

pro·trude (prō **trood′**) *v.* **pro·trud·ed, pro·trud·ing, pro·trudes.** To stick out or cause to stick out: *The jogger hit his head on a branch that protruded from a tree.*

pro·vi·sion (prə **vĭzh′** ən) *n.* **1.** The act of giving, providing, or supplying: *The students appreciated the provision of computers in all classrooms by the parent organization.* **2.** Something that is provided. **3. provisions.** Supplies of food and other necessities: *The astronauts had enough provisions for a ten-day space trip.*

pul·mo·nar·y (**pool′** mə nĕr′ ē *or* **pŭl′** mə nĕr′ ē) *adj.* Of, relating to, or affecting the lungs: *The pulmonary disease caused difficulty in breathing.*

pulse (pŭls) *n.* **1.** The regular expansion and contraction of the arteries caused by the beating of the heart as it pumps blood through them: *My pulse was rapid after the race.* **2.** A regular beating. —*v.* **pulsed, puls·ing, puls·es.** To beat regularly.

Q

quench (kwĕnch) *v.* **quenched, quench·ing, quench·es. 1.** To satisfy: *The canoe trip over the rapids did not quench my desire for adventure.* **2.** To put out; extinguish: *The rain quenched the forest fire.*

quis·ling (**kwĭz′** lĭng) *n.* A person who aids an invading enemy; traitor: *After the war the quisling was found guilty of treason.*

R

ra·di·ant (**rā′** dē ənt) *adj.* **1.** Giving off light or heat; shining brightly: *The radiant sunlight cheered the patients in the hospital.* **2.** Showing or filled with joy, happiness, pleasure, or brightness: *My brother's radiant smile indicated that he had been accepted to the summer camp.* **ra′ di·ant·ly** *adv.*

ran·sack (**răn′** săk′) *v.* To search through, damage, and leave in disorder in order to rob of valuables: *The thieves ransacked the jewelry store.*

rash·ly (**răsh′** lē) *adv.* Recklessly; hastily: *The mountain climbers acted rashly and did not take the necessary safety precautions.*

ra·tion (**răsh′** ən *or* **rā′** shən) *v.* To give out in fixed portions: *Water was rationed because of the severe drought.* —*n.* A fixed amount or share: *The refugee's ration of food was just enough.*

re·buff (rĭ **bŭf′**) *v.* To reject or drive away: *The army was able to rebuff the enemy.* —*n.* A blunt or sudden rejection or response: *My classmate's rebuff hurt my feelings.*

re·ces·sion (rĭ **sĕsh′** ən) *n.* **1.** The act of going back or away; withdrawal: *The recession of the glaciers at the end of the Ice Age took thousands of years.* **2.** An extended period of economic decline.

re·count (rĭ **kount′**) *v.* To tell in detail; relate; narrate: *The swimmer recounted her adventure of swimming across the English Channel.*

re·cu·per·a·tion (rĭ koo′ pə **rā′** shən) *n.* The act of gaining back health or strength; recovery: *My recuperation after the accident took a long time.*

ref·or·ma·tion (rĕf′ ər **mā′** shən) *n.* The act of changing, improving, or correcting by giving up harmful ways or defects: *The judge was amazed by the reformation of the criminal.*

re·fur·bish (rē **fûr′** bĭsh) *v.* **re·fur·bished, re·fur·bish·ing, re·fur·bish·es.** To make fresh and bright again; renovate: *Even though the old car runs well, the body needs to be refurbished.*

re·gen·er·ate (rĭ **jĕn′** ə rāt′) *v.* **re·gen·er·at·ed, re·gen·er·at·ing, re·gen·er·ates. 1.** To give new life, strength, or energy to; revive: *A vacation helps to regenerate a person's enthusiasm for work.* **2.** To grow again or replace: *Some animals are able to regenerate parts of their bodies.*

re·it·er·ate (rē **ĭt′** ə rāt′) *v.* **re·it·er·at·ed, re·it·er·at·ing, re·it·er·ates.** To say or do over again or repeatedly; repeat: *The teacher reiterated the instructions for the test.*

re·luc·tant (rĭ **lŭk′**tənt) *adj.* Unwilling: *The dog is reluctant to go down the stairs.* —**re·luc′tance** *n.* —**re·luc′tant·ly** *adv.*

re·peal (rĭ **pēl′**) *v.* To cancel or withdraw officially: *The judge ruled that the law violated the First Amendment and should be repealed.*

re·pug·nant (rĭ **pŭg′**nənt) *adj.* Causing dislike or disgust; offensive; distasteful: *The smell of the rotten oranges was repugnant.*

re·pulse (rĭ **pŭls′**) *v.* **re·pulsed, re·puls·ing, re·puls·es.** **1.** To drive back: *The offensive line of the football team was able to repulse the rival team on the third down.* **2.** To refuse to accept with rudeness: *The unfriendly girl repulsed her classmates' offer to join them at lunch.* —*n.* A rejection.

re·splen·dent (rĭ **splĕn′**dənt) *adj.* Dazzling; brilliant; beautiful; splendid: *The fireworks display was resplendent.*

res·to·ra·tion (rĕs′tə **rā′**shən) *n.* **1.** The act of bringing back to an original or former condition or state: *The restoration of the Sistine Chapel has taken years.* **2.** Something that is or has been brought back to an original condition: *We visited a restoration of a one-room schoolhouse.*

re·tail (**rē′**tāl′) *n.* The sale of goods in small amounts or individually directly to the public: *The retail of back-to-school items is profitable in August.*

S

sa·dis·tic (sə **dĭs′**tĭk) *adj.* Relating to or showing pleasure in being cruel: *The sadistic child likes to tease the hungry dog with food.*

sanc·tu·ar·y (**săngk′**choo ĕr′ē) *n., pl.* **sanc·tu·ar·ies.** **1.** A holy or sacred place, such as a church, temple, or mosque: *The worshipers were very quiet in the sanctuary.* **2.** A safe place: *The basement is a sanctuary during a tornado.* **3.** An area where animals are protected by law: *Animals are safe in the sanctuary because no hunting is allowed.*

scape·goat (**skāp′**gōt′) *n.* A person, group, or thing that unjustly bears the blame for the mistakes or wrongdoings of others: *The older brother was the scapegoat for the damage done by the younger brother.*

scath·ing (**skā′**thĭng) *adj.* Severely or harshly critical: *The scathing editorial criticized the mayor for closing the city hospital.*

scoff (skŏf *or* skôf) *v.* To express contempt for or make fun of as unimportant; ridicule; mock: *Some students scoff at the importance of good grades until they apply to colleges.* —*n.* A mocking expression.

scorn (skôrn) *v.* To refuse or reject because of a feeling that a person or thing is inferior or unworthy: *The girl scorned help from people she didn't respect.* —*n.* A strong feeling of dislike or contempt for a person or thing considered low, bad, or unworthy: *The man felt scorn for the person who lied to him.*

self-ef·fac·ing (sĕlf′ĭ **fā′**sĭng) *adj.* Keeping oneself in the background; modest: *Even though the actress won an Oscar, she was self-effacing.*

sen·ior·i·ty (sēn **yôr′**ĭ tē *or* sēn **yŏr′**ĭ tē) *n.* The state of being more advanced than others in age, rank, or length of service: *The teacher who had taught ten years had more seniority than the beginning teacher.*

ser·pen·tine (**sûr′**pən tēn′ *or* **sûr′**pən tīn′) *adj.* Having many bends and curves; winding like a snake's body: *We had to drive very slowly on the serpentine mountain road.*

sheep·ish (**shē′**pĭsh) *adj.* **1.** Embarrassed: *When Lisa realized her silly mistake, she gave a sheepish grin.* **2.** Shy; timid: *Nobody noticed his sheepish entrance into the room.* —**sheep′ish·ly** *adv.*

shrewd (shrood) *adj.* Clever, sharp, or quick-witted, especially in practical matters: *The shrewd politician was able to convince the voters that the popular law was her idea.* —**shrewd′ly** *adv.* —**shrewd′ness** *n.*

sin·ew (**sĭn′**yoo) *n.* A tough tissue that connects a muscle to a bone; tendon: *By exercising regularly I was able to improve the sinews in my upper arms.*

skep·ti·cal (**skĕp′**tĭ kəl) *adj.* Doubting; disbelieving: *The mother was skeptical of her daughter's excuse for being late.* —**skep′ti·cal·ly** *adv.*

slov·en·ly (**slŭv′**ən lē) *adj.* Untidy, sloppy, or careless, especially in dress or manner: *The child's slovenly appearance was an indication that something was wrong.*

slug·gish (**slŭg′**ĭsh) *adj.* **1.** Without energy, alertness, or vigor: *Sometimes too much sleep can make a person feel sluggish.* **2.** Slow: *The water is sluggish to drain from the sink.* —**slug′gish·ly** *adv.* —**slug′gish·ness** *n.*

snob·bish (**snŏb′**ĭsh) *adj.* Characteristic of a person who looks down on people that he or she considers as inferior in intelligence, wealth, achievement, or taste: *The snobbish girl made fun of her classmate's clothes.*

so·cia·ble (**sō′**shə bəl) *adj.* Liking to be with others; friendly: *By the end of the party, the sociable man knew all the other guests.* —**so′cia·bil′i·ty** *n.*

so·phis·ti·cat·ed (sə **fĭs**′tĭ kā′tĭd) *adj*. **1.** Highly complex; elaborate; complicated: *The sophisticated surgery was done with lasers.* **2.** Experienced and worldly-wise: *The sophisticated travelers ate at the best restaurants.*

sta·bil·i·ty (stə **bĭl**′ĭ tē) *n*., *pl*. **sta·bil·i·ties.** The condition or state of being firm; steadiness: *The highway department is concerned about the stability of old bridges.*

stat·u·esque (stăch′ o͞o **ĕsk**′) *adj*. Like a statue, as in size, dignity, and grace: *The statuesque pose of the model was very impressive.*

stim·u·late (**stĭm**′yə lāt′) *v*. **stim·u·lat·ed, stim·u·lat·ing, stim·u·lates.** To rouse or stir to greater action or effort: *The smell of my favorite food stimulates my appetite.*

stol·id (**stŏl**′ĭd) *adj*. **stol·id·er, stol·id·est.** Having or showing little or no emotion; unexcitable; impassive: *The defendant was stolid when the verdict was announced.*

stren·u·ous (**strĕn**′yo͞o əs) *adj*. Requiring or characterized by great effort or energy: *Everyone in the fitness class was tired after the strenuous workout.* **—stren′u·ous·ly** *adv*.

stu·pen·dous (sto͞o **pĕn**′dəs *or* styo͞o **pĕn**′dəs) *adj*. Of amazing excellence, force, volume, or degree; marvelous; tremendous; overwhelming: *The fans were awed by the stupendous distance of the homerun.* **—stu·pen′dous·ly** *adv*.

sub·con·scious (sŭb **kŏn**′shəs) *adj*. **1.** Existing in the mind, but the person is only partially aware that it is there: *Even though I had a lot to do, I had a subconscious wish to play.* **2.** Not completely conscious. **—***n*. The part of the mind that keeps experiences and feelings below the conscious level. **—sub·con′scious·ly** *adv*.

sub·due (səb **do͞o**′ *or* səb **dyo͞o**′) *v*. **sub·dued, sub·du·ing, sub·dues. 1.** To bring under control: *The zookeepers subdued the angry elephant.* **2.** To conquer: *The army troops subdued the enemy.* **3.** To lessen the intensity; tone down: *The parents asked their children to subdue their noise.*

sub·mis·sion (səb **mĭsh**′ən) *n*. The act of yielding or surrendering to the power or authority of another: *Germany's submission at the end of World War II ended the war in Europe.*

sub·or·di·nate (sə **bôr**′dn ĭt) *adj*. Lower in rank, importance, or order: *The salesman took a subordinate job because he needed money.* **—***n*. A person or thing that is less in rank, importance or order. **—***v*. (sə **bôr**′dn āt) To put in a place of lower rank, importance, or order.

sub·ser·vi·ent (səb **sûr**′vē ənt) *adj*. Overly willing to obey or yield to others: *The boss wanted the* employees to express themselves rather than be subservient. **—sub·ser′vi·ence** *n*.

sub·ver·sion (səb **vûr**′zhən *or* səb **vûr**′shən) *n*. The act of overthrowing or destroying something: *The traitors were arrested before they could carry out their planned subversion of the government.*

sul·len (**sŭl**′ən) *adj*. Sulky, withdrawn, or gloomy because of anger or a bad mood; glum: *Whenever the child didn't get his way, he became sullen.* **—sul′len·ly** *adv*. **—sul′len·ness** *n*.

su·per·fi·cial (so͞o′pər **fĭsh**′əl) *adj*. **1.** Being near the surface: *The superficial cut healed quickly.* **2.** Not thorough; shallow: *The audience was disappointed by the superficial interview with the mayor.* **—su′per·fi′ci·al′i·ty** *n*.

su·per·im·pose (so͞o′pər ĭm **pōz**′) *v*. **su·per·im·posed, su·per·im·pos·ing, su·per·im·pos·es.** To lay or place (something) over or on top of something else: *To show the correct answers, the teacher superimposed the answer key over the questions.*

su·per·la·tive (so͞o **pûr**′lə tĭv) *adj*. Superior to all others; of the highest degree: *Some gardeners think that roses are superlative flowers.*

su·per·nat·u·ral (so͞o′pər **năch**′ər əl) *adj*. Relating to existence beyond the power of the natural world, specifically involving something spiritual or divine: *Since there was not a scientific explanation for the bright light in the sky, the author gave a supernatural explanation.*

sym·me·try (**sĭm**′ĭ trē) *n*., *pl*. **sym·me·tries.** An exact arrangement so that parts are matching and balanced on either side of a central line: *The symmetry of the paintings is pleasing to the eye.*

symp·tom (**sĭm**′təm *or* **sĭmp**′təm) *n*. **1.** A sign or indication that a disease or disorder exists: *Weakness was the first symptom of the illness.* **2.** A sign or indication that something exists: *The big brown spot was a symptom that something was wrong with the lawn.*

syn·on·y·mous (sĭ **nŏn**′ə məs) *adj*. Having the same or very similar meaning: *The words* investigate *and* examine *are synonymous.*

T

tac·tic (**tăk**′tĭk) *n*. A plan for achieving a goal: *My tactic for getting into better shape is to walk two miles a day.*

tan·ta·lize (**tăn**′tə līz′) *v*. **tan·ta·lized, tan·ta·liz·ing, tan·ta·liz·es.** To tease by tempting with something desired but out of reach: *My friend likes to tantalize me by talking about food when I am hungry.*

tem·po·rar·y (tĕm′pə rĕr′ē) *adj.* Lasting for a limited time; not permanent: *The job was temporary and would last only for the summer.*

ten·den·cy (tĕn′dən sē) *n., pl.* **ten·den·cies. 1.** A trend or direction: *The tendency to use more convenience foods is growing.* **2.** A natural or usual inclination to act or behave in a certain way: *Latasha has a tendency to copy her older sister.*

tol·er·ate (tŏl′ə rāt′) *v.* **tol·er·at·ed, tol·er·at·ing, tol·er·ates. 1.** To accept; to put up with: *People who work in unskilled jobs may have to tolerate low salaries.* **2.** To allow; permit: *Teachers often tolerate lots of noise during recess.*

tran·si·to·ry (trăn′sĭ tôr′ē *or* trăn′zĭ tôr′ē) *adj.* Lasting only a short time; brief: *Even though the vacation was transitory, it was enjoyable.*

tril·o·gy (trĭl′ə jē) *n., pl.* **tril·o·gies.** A group of three related plays, operas, novels, or other dramatic or literary works that make up a series: *The author wrote a trilogy of mystery novels.*

tri·pod (trī′pŏd′) *n.* An adjustable three-legged stand or support: *I put the camera on a tripod so it would be stable.*

tri·um·vi·rate (trī ŭm′vər ĭt) *n.* Government by three persons who share authority, as in ancient Rome: *The triumvirate did not last because the three rulers did not trust each other.*

U

u·ni·fi·ca·tion (yōō′nə fĭ kā′shən) *n.* A joining together into a single unit: *The destruction of the Berlin Wall marked the unification of Germany.*

u·ni·lat·er·al (yōō′nə lăt′ər əl) *adj.* Of, affecting, or done by only one side: *The unilateral withdrawal of troops ended the conflict.* **—u′ni·lat′er·al·ly** *adv.*

u·nique (yōō nēk′) *adj.* **1.** One of a kind: *Each snowflake is unique.* **2.** Without an equal: *Shakespeare's plays and poems are unique.* **—u·nique′ly** *adv.* **—u·nique′ness** *n.*

u·ni·ver·sal (yōō′nə vûr′səl) *adj.* Present or existing everywhere: *Universal peace is a worthy goal.* **—u′ni·ver·sal′i·ty** *n.* **—u′ni·ver′sal·ly** *adv.*

un·ten·a·ble (ŭn tĕn′ə bəl) *adj.* Not capable of being supported or defended: *The girl realized that her argument was untenable.*

u·to·pi·an (yōō tō′pē ən) *adj.* **1.** Of, relating to, or like a perfect place where people live together in peace and happiness: *People would like to live in a utopian neighborhood.* **2.** Excellent or fine in theory but not possible or practical in reality.

V

ver·mil·ion (vər mĭl′yən) *n.* A bright red to reddish-orange color: *The beautiful bird had vermilion feathers.*

vin·dic·tive (vĭn dĭk′tĭv) *adj.* Showing or wanting revenge: *After the candidate lost the election, she was vindictive and said mean things about her opponent.* **—vin·dic′tive·ly** *adv.* **—vin·dic′tive·ness** *n.*

Standardized Test Practice

In lessons 1 to 36, you have concentrated on building vocabulary, a skill that is an important aid in reading comprehension. However, the competent reader must master a variety of other skills. These include the following:

- **Identifying main and subordinate ideas**—deciding what the most important idea in the selection is and what items support that idea

  Examples:

Main idea	The ancient Maya had a fascinating culture.
Subordinate	The ancient Maya developed irrigation.
	They created an accurate calendar.
	Mayan artists produced sculptures, painting, and jewelry.

- **Deciding on an appropriate title**—choosing a title that is closely related to the main idea of a selection

- **Drawing inferences**—coming to a conclusion that is not directly stated but is based on information given

  Example:

  If someone is breathing hard, you can infer that the person has been running.

- **Locating details**—scanning a selection to find the answer to a specific question

The following pages will give you a chance to practice the skills you use when you read. The questions they contain are the kinds of questions you will be asked to answer on a standardized test.

The reading selections include passages from science and social studies texts as well as informative essays and short narratives.

Reread the selection "The Headless Horseman of Sleepy Hollow" on page 1. Then circle the letter of the BEST choice to complete each statement.

1. Ichabod Crane was popular at parties because

   A. he was a very good dancer.

   B. he was a brilliant conversationalist.

   C. he was extremely strong and handsome.

   D. his teaching job would eventually make him wealthy.

2. Brom Bones played tricks on Ichabod because

   A. he wanted to amuse Katrina.

   B. he couldn't beat Ichabod in a fight.

   C. he considered Ichabod a rival to be scared away.

   D. the townspeople depended on Brom to get even with Ichabod.

3. It is NOT true that

   A. Brom Bones was in love with Katrina.

   B. the headless horseman threw his head at Ichabod.

   C. Ichabod left town because he was frightened and embarrassed.

   D. Ichabod believed the ghost stories that were told when the dance ended.

4. The word *invariably* means

   A. in different ways.

   B. without fail.

   C. usually.

   D. rarely.

5. A person who *ransacks* another's home

   A. leaves it in great disorder.

   B. leaves a wrapped gift there.

   C. listens in to private conversations.

   D. looks carefully for a hidden package.

Reread the selection "Autopsy" on page 71. Then circle the letter of the BEST choice to complete each statement.

1. In most cultures, the bodies of the dead are treated with
   A. abhorrence.
   B. indifference.
   C. great respect.
   D. reasonable care.

2. It is NOT true that
   A. doctors who perform autopsies are called pathologists.
   B. the early Chinese and Muslims were the first to perform autopsies.
   C. the dissection of corpses became scientifically acceptable during the Renaissance.
   D. after the invention of the microscope, autopsies could help to establish the causes of diseases and death.

3. Autopsies are important to the police because
   A. the treatment of our earthly remains is a matter of considerable importance.
   B. modern, scientifically sophisticated autopsies require comprehensive chemical analysis.
   C. an autopsy can often determine whether death was the result of foul play or of natural causes.
   D. until the nineteenth century, autopsies were limited to observations that could be made with the naked eye.

4. The word *remains*, as used in the first paragraph, means
   A. a corpse.
   B. a monument.
   C. an inheritance.
   D. a cemetery plot.

5. Something that has *significance*, according to the last paragraph,
   A. is proof of foul play.
   B. may be a sign or an omen.
   C. is text intended for a street sign.
   D. has meaning that may not be obvious.

Reread the selection "The Siege of Vicksburg" on page 99. Then circle the letter of the BEST choice to complete each statement.

1. The word *severed,* in the first paragraph, means

   A. cut off.

   B. acquired.

   C. led away.

   D. strictly followed.

2. The word *entrenched,* as used in the first paragraph, means

   A. in foxholes.

   B. well situated.

   C. in clear view.

   D. highly entertained.

3. In securing the surrender of Vicksburg, Ulysses S. Grant showed

   A. bravery and charity.

   B. honesty and strength.

   C. perseverance and ingenuity.

   D. intelligence and dependability.

4. The citizens of Vicksburg did not celebrate the Fourth of July for many years because

   A. Pemberton surrendered Vicksburg to Union Forces on July 4, 1863.

   B. it did not have the resources necessary for a big celebration.

   C. the inhabitants of the city had too much work to do.

   D. they held a separate celebration just for the city.

5. While Grant attacked Vicksburg from the west,

   A. some of his troops attacked from the north.

   B. the Confederate forces retreated southward.

   C. many of the Confederate soldiers hid in the swamp.

   D. Sherman blocked escape and supply routes on the east.

6. Pemberton was forced to surrender because

   A. his troops did not have enough ammunition.

   B. his troops were fighting among themselves.

   C. the civilian inhabitants of Vicksburg were starving.

   D. he was exhausted from the struggle against Union forces.

Reread the article "Fossils Trapped in Tar" on page 155. Then circle the letter of the BEST choice to complete each statement.

1. The word *ooze,* as used in the first paragraph, means

   A. oil seepage.

   B. soft mud or slime.

   C. a byproduct of ozone.

   D. egg-producing animals.

2. One inference that can be drawn from the account is that

   A. tens of thousands of years ago, conditions in what is now Los Angeles supported hundreds of animal species.

   B. the Los Angeles area has extremely cold winters and hot summers.

   C. the remains of many hunters were found in the tar pits.

   D. the study of fossils is usually a waste of time.

3. The Rancho La Brea tar pits are MOST important because

   A. they supply glue for use in industry.

   B. they attract thousands of tourists to the area.

   C. the information that they supply about the past may provide clues to the future.

   D. the area has ideal conditions for use as an animal preserve for endangered species.

4. One beneficial effect of the tar in the pits was that

   A. it caused the death of thousands of animals.

   B. it preserved the bones of animals as fossils.

   C. it prevented the erosion of the surface.

   D. petroleum can be extracted from it.

5. A *paleontologist* studies

   A. palace building.

   B. Caucasian origins.

   C. the causes of albinism.

   D. prehistoric forms of life.

Read the passage below and answer the questions that follow. Remember that the time and place of a story may be revealed indirectly through descriptive passages.

from "If I Forget Thee, O Earth . . . "

by Arthur C. Clarke

1   When Marvin was ten years old, his father took him through the long, echoing corridors that led up through Administration and Power, until at last they came to the uppermost levels of all and were among the swiftly growing vegetation of the Farmlands.

2   Marvin liked it here: it was fun watching the great, slender plants creeping with almost visible eagerness toward the sunlight as it filtered down through the plastic domes to meet them. The smell of life was everywhere, awakening inexpressible longings in his heart: no longer was he breathing the dry, cool air of the residential levels, purged of all smells but the faint tang of ozone. He wished he could stay here for a little while, but Father would not let him.

3   They went onward until they had reached the entrance to the Observatory, which he had never visited: but they did not stop, and Marvin knew with a sense of rising excitement that there could be only one goal left. For the first time in his life, he was going Outside.

Choose the BEST answer for each multiple-choice question. Circle the letter that comes before each correct answer.

1.   Where does this story take place?

   A. in an office building

   B. on a campground with caves

   C. on a farm that has many buildings

   D. in a residential area that is mostly underground

2.   In what time is this story set?

   A. the future

   B. the distant past

   C. a town in another country

   D. a park in the United States

3. What does Marvin see when he and his father arrive at the highest level?

   A. sunlight

   B. small animals and insects

   C. powerful men and women

   D. offices of the Administration

4. What does the last line of the passage tell the reader about Marvin's surroundings?

   A. Marvin lives on a farm.

   B. Marvin loves to be outdoors.

   C. Marvin has never been outdoors.

   D. Marvin's family lives far from other families.

5. What Marvin sees helps the reader understand the places through which he and his father pass. What other sense does the author use to describe the setting?

   A. taste

   B. smell

   C. touch

   D. sound

6. Why would the story about Marvin interest most readers? Choose the most important reason.

   A. Readers like stories about fathers and sons.

   B. Readers know people like Marvin and his father.

   C. Readers understand the excitement of seeing things grow.

   D. Readers are curious about the possibility of living on other planets.

7. What does the word *purged,* in paragraph 2, mean?

   A. wasted

   B. reeking

   C. cleansed

   D. composed

Read the following paragraphs and complete the statements that follow. Circle the letter that comes before the BEST choice.

The Appalachian Trail runs more than twenty-one hundred miles in the eastern United States through the Appalachian Mountains. Ambling across ranges with interesting names such as Blue Ridge, Smoky, and Catskill Mountains, the trail wanders between Georgia and Maine. It passes through fourteen states. About two hundred people each year hike the trail from end to end, braving its hardships to experience its beauty.

1. The purpose of this passage is to

   A. persuade the reader to hike the Trail.

   B. explain how to hike the Appalachian Trail.

   C. provide facts, for the reader, about the Appalachian Trail.

   D. describe some natural beauty in the eastern United States.

2. This passage was written for people who

   A. are from either Georgia or Maine.

   B. are interested in learning about places to hike.

   C. are interested in the history of the eastern United States.

   D. know everything there is to know about the Appalachian Trail.

Don't embark on a camping expedition without knowing what conditions to expect and without being adequately prepared to meet them. Basic equipment includes a knapsack, a tent, and a sleeping bag. For information on the wide variety of knapsacks available and the way to determine which knapsack is right for you, see chapter 2. For further information on purchasing tents and sleeping bags, see chapter 4.

3. The purpose of this passage is to

   A. inform people of what to bring when camping.

   B. entertain the reader with stories about camping.

   C. illustrate the difference between camping and hiking.

   D. encourage retail stores to sell certain kinds of equipment.

4. This passage is meant to appeal to people who

   A. hate the outdoors.

   B. are expert campers.

   C. want to try camping.

   D. need to know where to shop for camping supplies.

Read the passage below and complete the statements that follow.

The Difficulties of Development

In the Front Range, an area along the foothills of Colorado's Rocky Mountains, the population is rising. As a result, more and more countryside is being developed for residential use. Residential expansion in the region has been too rapid to be well planned. Traffic between cities is now bumper to bumper. In some areas, wells have gone dry because of the water demands created by the new developments.

The increase in the human population has created a life-threatening situation for the animals of the Front Range. Several elk are killed by cars each year because residential developments are encroaching on some traditional elk feeding grounds. Developments have deprived cougars of a place to rear their offspring. Recently a cougar and her cubs were seen on a hospital patio. The migration patterns of elk and deer have also been disrupted.

Although there are no obvious solutions to the problems of this situation, there are ways to minimize the damage it causes. One way to decrease the amount of land required to accommodate the increasing population is to build multiunit homes.

Circle the letter of the BEST choice to complete the statement.

1. The main idea of this article is that

   A. balancing human and animal needs is problematic.

   B. animal needs are more important than human needs.

   C. human needs are more important than animal needs.

   D. animals are being harmed by development of the Front Range.

2. The main idea of the first paragraph is an explanation of

   A. the history of the Front Range.

   B. the reasons the area is called the Front Range.

   C. the causes and effects of development.

   D. how animals are being harmed by development.

3. The main idea of the second paragraph is a discussion of

   A. where to build residences.

   B. how animals are being threatened.

   C. why hunting is a bad practice.

   D. how to solve the Front Range problem.

4. The main idea of the third paragraph concerns

   A. recent research efforts.

   B. where development is taking place.

   C. the people of the Front Range.

   D. how to solve the Front Range problem.

Read the selection below and then answer the questions that follow.

Tyrone and the Cheesecake

1   That night, when Tyrone went home, he got out his recipe books and spent the evening looking them over. He decided that he would make an orange crunch cheesecake and the New York cheesecake that he had mentioned to his friends at lunch. He also decided that it would be much more fun to bake with a friend. At lunch the next day, he brought up the cheesecake contest again, but this time he had a different attitude.

2   "I've still got cheesecake on my mind," said Tyrone, "and I think I'd really have my hands full trying to bake two cakes by myself. Would anyone like to lend a hand? I think it'll be fun."

3   At first his friends looked skeptical, but Destiny leaned forward with her sandwich in hand and said, "Yeah, Tyrone, I've been wanting to learn to bake. That New York cheesecake sounds tasty. I'll help."

4   Tyrone was sure that, with Destiny's help, baking two delicious cakes would be simple. The evening before the contest, the two met at Tyrone's house to make a shopping list. Destiny wondered why Tyrone had left this to the eleventh hour, but she didn't say anything.

5   At the store, Tyrone and Destiny filled their cart with eggs, raspberries, oranges, sugar, cream cheese, and graham crackers.

6   "Okay, let's get a move on," said Tyrone when they walked through the door of his house. Destiny started measuring ingredients. Tyrone preheated the oven.

7.   "Easy does it on the orange rind," Destiny warned, as she watched Tyrone add the grated orange to the batter. The hours went by and it started to get dark outside. Destiny began to wonder whether they would have time to make two cakes. But Tyrone seemed to be enjoying himself, and soon the first cake went into the oven. The kitchen started to smell really good. Destiny knew they were in the home stretch.

Circle the letter of the BEST choice to complete each statement.

1. When the selection says that Tyrone "looked over" his recipe books, it means that he

    A. read them.

    B. did not read them.

    C. looked at the covers.

    D. looked above them at something that caught his eye.

2. When Tyrone says "I've still got cheesecake on my mind," he means that he is

    A. ready for dinner.   C. thinking about cheesecake.

    B. covered in cheesecake   D. sorry for the way he acted yesterday.

3. When Tyrone asks his friends whether anyone would like to "lend a hand," he is asking them

    A. to shake his hand.

    B. to help him bake the cakes.

    C. to tell him whether anyone has ever baked before.

    D. to taste the cakes when they are done baking.

4. The phrase "the eleventh hour," in paragraph 4, means

    A. at 11 o'clock.

    B. at dinner time.

    C. at the last minute.

    D. at exactly the right time.

5. The phrase "get a move on," in paragraph 6, means

    A. go to the store.

    B. take it easy.

    C. eat dinner.

    D. hurry up.

6. When Destiny knows that they are "in the home stretch," she knows that

    A. they are almost done.

    B. the cakes will be great.

    C. they will be cooking all night.

    D. they need to stretch out before cooking the next cake.

7. When Destiny says "easy does it on the orange rind," she wants Tyrone to

    A. pass her an orange.

    B. peel the orange to remove the rind.

    C. put no more orange rind into the batter.

    D. put some more eggs into the cake batter.

8. The word *skeptical,* in paragraph 3, means.

    A. afraid.

    B. certain.

    C. worried.

    D. doubtful.

Read the selection below and answer the questions that follow it.

Breaking the Silence

1   Lisa dumped her overnight bag onto the floor of her grandmother's guest room and gazed out the window. The trip, all three hours of it, had been largely a silent one. Lisa had pretended to nap so as to forestall conversation, and she had been successful. Now she would pretend to unpack until her mother's car turned onto the country road and disappeared.

2   Lisa and her mother usually managed to get along. There were arguments about what was "suitable attire" for school, how late Lisa could stay out, and what her chores were. But none of these disagreements had seriously threatened their ability to coexist. The latest disagreement did.

3   The problem had begun a week ago when Lisa's mother had informed her that they would not be going to the beach on their summer vacation. This year Lisa would not have that precious time she looked forward to while she listened to the petty gossip of the people she called her friends. There would be no long walks with her cousin Mara during which they would share their real feelings about everything. There would be no swimming races, bike rides, or luxurious hours of sun and sand. And why not? Because there were "other things" they needed the money for. Other things! What other things could possibly be important enough to eliminate the only thing Lisa really cared about?

4   She responded with a cold "Bye!" when her mother called, "I'll see you Sunday night." Lisa waited to hear the car door slam before she left the room. If she could enlist her grandmother's help, maybe it would still be possible to change her mother's mind. That is why her first remark when she walked into the kitchen was "You know how much Mara and I like seeing each other every summer? Well, this year, Mom canceled our vacation plans."

5   Her grandmother looked at her with a strange expression on her face. "Yes . . . I know," she replied. "That's too bad."

6   "But, why?" said Lisa. "Why isn't this trip important to her? It is to me!"

7   Her grandmother sighed. "I'm sure your mother knows what she's doing," she said. Then, making it clear that she was not going to discuss the issue, Grandmother said, "If you pick a quart of strawberries, I'll make shortcake for dessert."

8   So Lisa crawled along the rows of low-growing plants, feeling the sun on her back and searching for berries that had reached their perfect ripeness. It was not hard to find a quart; and when the basket was full, she carried it into the house and put it on the kitchen counter. Her grandmother was in the front yard, weeding the flower garden. Lisa would normally have gone outside to help. She liked helping her grandmother because she and her grandmother always talked while they worked.

Lisa told stories about school and friends and confessed her worries and planned her future, and her grandmother listened and laughed in the right places and never in the wrong ones. But if her grandmother was going to take Lisa's mother's side . . .

9   Lisa wandered into the study to find a book. She spotted the glow of the computer. There would not be any good games on it because her grandmother used it almost exclusively for e-mail, but there might be solitaire. Instead she decided to send an e-mail message to Mara. Mara understood. Mara was on her side, even if no one else was.

10   When Lisa tapped the mouse to get rid of the screen saver, her grandmother's e-mail inbox listings appeared. Lisa saw her own recent messages and several messages from her mother. The latest message from her mother was identified with the subject "Surgery date." Surgery date? What surgery? Reading other people's mail was not something Lisa would ordinarily do, but this was different. Surgery date! She double-clicked on the words, and a message appeared.

11   Hey, Mom, the surgery is on for the 16th. Now that it's definite, I'll have to tell Lisa—maybe after this weekend. She's still furious that we're not going to the beach this summer. I'll have to explain, but it took her so long to get over losing her father that I can hardly bear to tell her that now her mother's sick too. I still haven't gathered the courage to tell her what I need to use the vacation money for. What a coward I am! As you surely remember, dealing with an angry teenager is just a part of life. Comparatively speaking, it's easy! I'd rather have her be angry than scared.

12   I'll drop her off Friday morning and pick her up Sunday night. Have a good weekend, OK? Make her some of your strawberry shortcake. That always cheered me up!

13   Lisa's heart thudded painfully. She closed her eyes and was, quite suddenly, four years old again and lost at the amusement park. She could hear the jangling, jarring music and the sounds of children shrieking. A hollow feeling clutched at her stomach—nothing would ever be right again. There were people everywhere, laughing and calling to each other. None of them were paying the slightest attention to the small silent child they jostled in their hurry. The colors were too bright, the noises too loud, the place too big and full of strangers. She had to find her mother, had to, had to! And she ran, searching, searching . . .

14   Lisa shook herself. She was not four years old; she was fourteen. She would breathe deeply and . . . and what? It had been—she glanced at her watch—about an hour since her mother left. The cell phone would be on the front seat of the car. Lisa could reach her mother, could hear her mother's voice. She blinked the tears out of her eyes and dialed. When her mother answered, Lisa forced calm into her voice and said, "Mom, you have to tell me about the surgery. Pull over, stop the car, and tell me now."

15   Her mother told her. It was all going to be hard, and it would change everything for a while, but she was not going to die. She promised, and Lisa believed her. When Lisa thought about it, missing a vacation at the beach was a matter of no importance at all.

¹⁶ Lisa walked out into the sunlight of the yard. "Mom's coming back," she said. "She's going to spend the weekend with us."

¹⁷ Her grandmother looked up in surprise. "She is? That's wonderful! But . . . why?"

¹⁸ "Oh," said Lisa, leaning over and yanking out a weed, "I asked her to. I . . . I suddenly missed her. And, besides, she really likes your strawberry shortcake."

Circle the letter of the BEST choice to answer each question.

1. What is this selection mainly about?

   A. how a person finds the courage to do what is necessary

   B. how information helps someone realize what is important

   C. how the loss of something can make that object more valuable

   D. how difficult seeing the world through another person's eyes can be

2. In paragraph 1, what does the word *forestall* mean?

   A. prevent

   B. drag out

   C. encourage

   D. participate in

3. In paragraph 8, why does Lisa decide not to help her grandmother in the garden?

   A. She is angry with her mother.

   B. She does not enjoy gardening.

   C. She is irritated with her grandmother.

   D. She wants to talk to her mother on the phone.

4. Which sentence from the selection introduces a flashback?

   A. "Lisa would normally have gone outside to help."

   B. "The trip, all three hours of it, had been largely a silent one."

   C. "She closed her eyes and was, quite suddenly, four years old again and lost at the amusement park."

   D. "This year Lisa would not have that precious time she looked forward to while she listened to the petty gossip of the people she called her friends."

5. In paragraph 10, why does Lisa read the e-mail message from her mother?

   A. She cannot find anything else to read.

   B. She is curious about the subject of the message.

   C. She and her mother always read each other's mail.

   D. She wants to know whether her mother has been complaining about her.

6. What is Lisa's first reaction to the message?

   A. fear

   B. guilt

   C. anger

   D. sympathy

7. What does the message reveal to the reader that the rest of the story, limited to Lisa's point of view, could not?

   A. who Mara is

   B. why Lisa is so angry

   C. why the vacation was canceled

   D. when the problem between Lisa and her mother began

8. What has Lisa's mother been hesitant to do?

   A. argue with Lisa

   B. have a needed operation

   C. go on a vacation to the beach

   D. tell Lisa about the necessary surgery

9. When does Lisa's attitude change?

   A. when she discovers that her mother is ill

   B. when she uses her grandmother's computer

   C. when she sends an e-mail message to Mara

   D. when she helps her grandmother pick strawberries

10. What mood does the author's choice of words in paragraph 13 create?

    A. panic

    B. regret

    C. loneliness

    D. excitement

11. Which sentence from the selection shows the reader that Lisa does not know all there is to know about the canceled vacation plans?

    A. "Mara was on her side, even if no one else was."

    B. "I'm sure your mother knows what she's doing."

    C. "Because there were 'other things' they needed the money for."

    D. "Her grandmother looked at her with a strange expression on her face."

12. Which sentence from the selection represents an opinion?

    A. "Lisa's heart thudded painfully."

    B. "Mara was on her side, even if no one else was."

    C. "The trip, all three hours of it, had been largely a silent one."

    D. "The problem had begun a week ago when Lisa's mother had informed her that they would not be going to the beach on their summer vacation."

Word	Lesson	Word	Lesson	Word	Lesson
abdicate	24	bicentennial	12	eminent	28
abhor	24	bicker	35	emission	33
abhorrent	16	biennial	14	enchanted	1
abomination	24	bilateral	20	encompass	34
aborigines	24	bilingual	12	encumbrance	25
abort	24	biome	25	enhance	19
abound	19	blasphemy	35	ensure	28
abrasive	24	blighted	32	eradicate	21
abrupt	24	bovine	8	erosion	21
absolute	24	brawny	1	esophagus	29
abstain	24	breach	13	estrange	21
abuse	24	bulbous	20	etiquette	13
accentuate	30	cajole	28	evolve	21
accolade	7	camouflage	25	exacerbate	21
accomplished	1	capillary	29	excavate	34
acquiescence	30	citadel	22	excel	21
acquisition	30	classic	31	execute	31
addendum	19	cleave	10	expansion	4
admonish	30	clergy	11	expatriate	21
advent	30	coerce	35	expedient	22
adversary	30	cohesive	10	expel	3
affiliate	30	colleague	7	extensive	7
affirm	30	comely	32	exterminate	21
affix	30	compel	3	extinct	21
affliction	30	compound interest	26	extremity	21
agonize	28	comprehensive	16	exuberant	2
alienate	13	concave	20	ferret	25
ambidextrous	12	confute	34	fervid	34
ambivalent	12	congeal	34	fickle	10
amicable	2	congestion	34	flexible	4
amorous	1	contrived	19	forage	25
anecdote	28	convex	20	foreclose	26
antagonize	13	cosigner	26	formidable	22
antebellum	15	creditor	26	fury	7
antecedent	15	cultural	13	garner	7
antedate	15	dank	25	generation	6
anteroom	15	dappled	25	genetic	6
anticlimax	15	debit	26	genial	6
antidote	15	decrepit	32	gentry	6
antipathy	15	default	26	geometric	36
antiseptic	15	defiant	2	germinate	6
antisocial	15	demise	34	human	14
antitoxin	15	desecration	16	humane	14
appeal	3	designation	33	hyperactive	9
appraise	26	despise	10	hyperbole	9
apprentice	5	despondent	2	hyperextension	9
aptitude	5	devastate	7	hypersonic	9
assets	26	differentiate	16	hypertension	9
asunder	22	disdain	10	hypochondriac	9
automation	4	disgruntled	2	hypocrisy	9
awe	28	disguise	1	hypodermic	9
babel	23	disintegrate	10	hypotenuse	9
badger	8	disparity	19	hypothetical	9
banter	35	dissection	16	ignition	33
basilica	11	dogged	8	immerse	34
bastion	22	dominate	4	immortal	6
beastly	8	drab	32	impair	19
bedeck	1	drudgery	5	impassive	19
berserk	2	egotistical	17	implore	31
beseech	35	eliminate	13	impromptu	28
biannual	14	elliptical	20	impulse	3

Word	Lesson	Word	Lesson	Word	Lesson
inarticulate	27	mold	10	sadistic	23
incarceration	10	moral	14	sanctuary	11
inclement	27	morale	14	scapegoat	8
inconspicuous	27	mortality	6	scathing	35
indignant	17	mortician	6	scoff	35
indiscreet	27	mosque	11	scorn	35
induction	33	mullah	11	self-effacing	17
influential	36	mundane	32	seniority	5
insignificant	4	mutation	16	serpentine	20
intently	28	narcissism	23	sheepish	8
invariably	1	nepotism	5	shrewd	28
inversion	33	neutralize	22	sinew	29
invulnerable	27	offensive	13	skeptical	17
irrational	27	originate	31	slovenly	32
irredeemable	27	orthopedic	29	sluggish	8
irrefutable	27	pallid	32	snobbish	17
irrelevant	27	pandemonium	23	sociable	17
irretrievable	27	parasitic	36	sophisticated	16
journeyman	5	peal	3	stability	25
jovial	23	perilous	7	statuesque	20
Koran	11	personified	31	stimulate	19
kosher	11	pervade	34	stolid	17
laborious	5	physique	1	strenuous	36
lackey	5	pitfalls	13	stupendous	25
lackluster	32	polygon	20	subconscious	18
laggard	5	postmortem	6	subdue	18
laity	11	potential	13	submission	18
lame duck	8	preponderance	4	subordinate	18
lampoon	35	primarily	7	subservient	18
larcenous	36	probe	34	subversion	18
larynx	29	proliferation	19	sullen	17
lascivious	2	prominent	31	superficial	18
lecherous	36	prompt	10	superimpose	18
lesion	29	propel	3	superlative	18
lethal	16	proportion	31	supernatural	18
liability	26	propulsion	3	symmetry	20
liberation'	33	protrude	1	symptom	16
lien	26	provision	33	synonymous	36
ligament	29	pulmonary	29	tactic	22
Lilliputian	23	pulse	3	tantalize	23
limerick	23	quench	10	temporary	4
linear	20	quisling	23	tendency	4
lionize	8	radiant	32	tolerate	4
loathsome	2	ransack	1	transaction	26
luxuriant	25	rashly	7	transitory	7
mammoth	8	ration	22	trilogy	12
maniacal	36	rebuff	22	tripod	12
manuscript	28	recession	33	triumvirate	12
marital	14	recount	19	unification	12
marrow	29	recuperation	33	unilateral	12
martial	14	reformation	33	unique	12
mecca	11	refurbish	31	universal	13
meddle	14	regenerate	6	untenable	22
meddlesome	2	reiterate	35	utopian	23
medicinal	36	reluctant	17	vermilion	31
melancholy	2	repeal	3	vindictive	17
menial	5	repugnant	16		
menorah	11	repulse	3		
metabolism	29	resplendent	32		
metallic	36	restoration	31		
mettle	14	retail	4		